SIX SIGMA HANDBOOK

A Complete Step-by-step Guide to Understanding

(A Complete Guide - Gain Benefits in Your Business and Your Job)

Carolyn Sandberg

GW00567335

Published by Tomas Edwards

Six Sigma Handbook: A Complete Step-by-step Guide to Understanding (A Complete Guide - Gain Benefits in Your Business and Your Job)

ISBN 978-1-989744-90-1

LEGAL & DISCLAIMER

The information contained in this book is not designed to replace or take the place of any form of medicine or professional medical advice. The information in this book has been provided for educational and entertainment purposes only.

The information contained in this book has been compiled from sources deemed reliable, and it is accurate to the best of the Author's knowledge; however, the Author cannot guarantee its accuracy and validity and cannot be held liable for any errors or omissions. Changes are periodically made to this book. You must consult your doctor or get professional medical advice before using any of the suggested remedies, techniques, or information in this book.

Upon using the information contained in this book, you agree to hold harmless the Author from and against any damages, costs, and expenses, including any legal fees potentially resulting from the application of any of the information provided by this guide. This disclaimer applies to any damages or injury caused by the use and application, whether directly or indirectly, of any advice or information presented, whether for breach of contract, tort, negligence, personal injury, criminal intent, or under any other cause of action.

You agree to accept all risks of using the information presented inside this book. You need to consult a professional medical practitioner in order to ensure you are both able and healthy enough to participate in this program.

Table of Contents

Introduction

There are two questions that any company can ask to both reduce unnecessary failure while at the same time ensuring that the company focuses only on ideas that have promising potential. They are:

Should we build this new service or product?

How can we improve our odds of success with this new thing?

The Lean method is equally useful for startup companies as it is for Fortune 500 companies. It may have its roots in the technology sector but it is already being used in virtually every industry across the board. While there is lots of confusion around it, the Lean Startup system can help companies of all sizes in a lot of different ways.

While the term "startup" generally has very specific connotations in the business world, in this instance, "startup" simply means any team that is planning to create a new product or service whose future isn't 100 percent certain yet. Generally speaking, it makes far more sense to classify startups as enterprises taking on the challenge amidst uncertainty, than by categories like market sector, size or even age of the company.

With this definition in mind, you will find that there are a few main areas in which a startup faces the greatest amount of uncertainty, otherwise known as risk. Technical or product risk can be summed up by the question "Can it be built?" As an example, doctors who are currently working towards a cure for cancer can be thought of as a startup institution because there is a very large technical risk and this area of study has been going on for quite some time with no hint of success. However, if they do discover a cure, there is absolutely no market risk because its target market would definitely buy it.

Market risk, also known as customer risk, is simply the risk when the product or service reaches the market and no one is actually going to want to buy it. A cautionary example of this type of risk is a company named Webvan that spent millions and millions of dollars creating an automated means of buying groceries online. The only problem is that they tried to get this system up and running in the early 2000s. This is a time when many people were still getting comfortable with the concept of the internet in general but the comfort in buying everyday products online did not follow until nearly a decade.

The business model risk is the risk associated with taking a good idea and building a functioning business plan around it. Even if you already have a good idea, the right business model could very well not be visible until the service is up and running. As an example, when Google started its original business plan of selling advertisements based on previous searches, the plan wasn't clear because no one had done that sort of thing before.

While every company will need to deal with these risks to varying degrees, the biggest risk that most new products or services struggle with is customer risk. It can be difficult to determine the value of something new for customers who haven't experienced it yet. The tricky part here is that in most instances, it will actually appear that the product risk is the most urgent risk. After all, most new ideas don't make it this far without an assumption that someone, somewhere is going to want the product or service at hand. This assumption, then, can lead to a much costlier course of action wherein you do the work to create the product or service before offering it to anyone.

This is where the Lean Startup system comes into play. This technology potentially stops you from being one of the millions of companies out there that has a good idea and a cool product but had crashed and burned because they inherently relied on assumptions about consumer behavior that simply turned out not be true. It is important to think in terms of risk as opposed to company history because in doing so, you will find that many large companies have startup organizations within them. As an example, consider the Gillette razor company who felt that there was little risk in adding the fifth blade to their flagship line of razors because they knew the business model, the market, and the product ins and outs. However, the company that owns Gillette, Proctor and Gamble, operates a startup in the form of its research and development division that focuses specifically on hair removal. With each new idea, this division seems like a startup because they have no known variable which means everything they are working on is extremely risky.

Currently, one of the well-known companies that using the Lean Startup system is General Electric, which is also one of the largest companies in the world.

The company has trained more than 10,000 managers around the world to use Lean Startup principles and has used the system to successfully improve the end result on all of their products including refrigerators and diesel engines.

To follow in their footsteps, the following chapters will discuss how to operate a Lean Startup successfully, starting with an overview of the Lean Startup methodology. Next, you will learn how to create a trial startup system that is not only useful but also designed to provide you with as much viable information as possible. You will then learn how to take a successful startup and grow it until it reaches its full potential. From there you will learn about adding Six Sigma and other Lean tools to your startup for maximum efficacy.

Chapter 1: What Is Six Sigma?

If you have been running your business for some time, you have probably heard about Six Sigma at some point. It is known as a quality improvement method that is used often to help youfind defects in the business model so that you can reduce them and get the business to be more effective than before.

Six Sigma is one of the most effective methods currently available to help improve the performance of any organization. It is able to do this by minimizing the defects in a business's products or service. With this method, all the errors committed have a cost associated in the form of losing customers, replacing a part, waste of material or time, redoing a task, or missing efficiency. In the end, this could end up costing the business. Six Sigma works to reduce these losses in order to help a business grow.

This methodology of Six Sigma was endorsed by Motorola in the 1980s. The company, at that time, was trying to find a way that they could measure their defects at a granular level compared to the previous methods, and their hope was to reduce these defects in order to provide a better product to their customers.

What they ended up with was a huge increase in the quality levels of several of their products, and the company received the first Malcolm Baldrige National Quality Award. It did not take long until Motorola shared their Six Sigma method and soon there were many other companies who were reaping the rewards as well. By 2003, it was estimated that the combined savings of all companies using the Six Sigma method were more than $100 billion.

What is the Sigma Scale?

The first thing that we are going to look at is known as the Sigma scale. This is a universal measure of the performance of any type of organization or business. Sigma is known as the statistical term to represent a standard deviation or the measure of a variation in a dataset. Higher scores of this indicate better performance, or it can mean the results are more precise.

In other words, if the output is defective 60 percent of the time, it means that the performance of One Sigma is compliant. However, if the output is defective 31 percent of the time, it means that it is demonstrating what is known as Two Sigma compliance. An example of how this works for the different Sigma's includes the following table:

The Sigma Scale		
Sigma	Percent Defective	Defects out of a Million
1	69%	691,462
2	31%	308,538

3	6.70%	66,807
4	.062%	6,210
5	0.02%	233
6	0.00%	3.4
7	0.00%	0.019

As shown above, Six Sigma implies almost perfect output because there are only 3.4 defects per million opportunities.

DPMO

The term defect is used a lot when it comes to Six Sigma. The goal of the company is to reduce how many defects occur so they can reduce waste, provide a better product for their company, and make more money. However, what does this defect mean?

The "defect" is going to be explained as the nonconformities that are showing up in an output that falls lower than what the customers find as satisfactory. The number of DPMO, or defects present per million opportunities, is going to be used to figure out which part of the Sigma scale that process corresponds to. Most organizations in the world would fall somewhere between Three and Four Sigma. This may not seem so bad, but it really implies that they could be losing up to a quarter of their total revenue simply because there are some defects in the organization.

The Six Sigma methodology can help these businesses out. It can move them up to a new level of Sigma, which can reduce all that waste and those defects, effectively helping them to earn more profits.

Applying Six Sigma

While there are many different methodologies that can come with Six Sigma and can help the business to reduce its defects, the two basic ones that are good to start with include DFSS and DMAIC. Let us look at each of them below to understand how they work a little better.

DMAIC

The first one is DMAIC. In order to help modify a process that is already in existence and change it so that it can be more compliant with the Six Sigma methodology, therefore, more efficient, you would work with DMAIC. This stands for:

Define: This is where an organization needs to define the goals for process improvements so that they are in coherence with the strategies of the business and with the demands of the customers. You can't get far in your process without defining what goals you want to reach and which processes must be improved to reach these goals.

Measure: This is the current performance of the systems in place for the business. It will also take some time to gather data that is relevant and can be used in the future. Measuring the data you receive and the results that you are looking for can be important, and you must make sure you are relying on the right tools to do it.

Analyze: This is where you will analyze the current setting and then observe how the relationship between the performance and the key parameters work. Lean analytics can be a good tool to use to analyze the situation and make sure your improvements are actually working. If changes need to be made, your analysis will showcase when this should happen.

Improve: From the other steps, you will be able to find ways to improve the process. This helps to optimize the process to earn the business more money.

Control: Here you will control the parameters before they are able to affect the outcome.

DFSS

Now, the business can also choose to completely start a new process from scratch and make it work with the Six Sigma methodology. This would be done with DFSS. When a new process is started in this manner, Design for Six Sigma methodology, or DFSS, is going to be used. Some see it just as an offshoot of Six Sigma and others are going to see it as its own methodology. Either way, the DFSS requires the IDOV approach, which stands for:

Identify: Here you are going to identify and then define the process goals. These need to be consistent with both the standards of your industry as well as the demands of the customer.

Design: This includes taking into consideration all of the possible solutions, and then selecting the one that is optimal.

Optimize: This is when you will optimize the performance of the application. You can use different methods to do this such as statistical modeling and advanced simulations.

Validate: This is when you will verify the solution that you chose and see if it works.

There are times when the DMAIC that we talked about before can turn into a DFSS. This happens when you look at the processes you are using and find they are completely irrelevant or just are not working for you. You may decide to redesign them to get the results that you want.

For some people, they want to be able to use the system that they already have in place to get started with Six Sigma. Others find that how they currently do things is such a mess that it is just easier to start over and try something new. Your business will have to look at its current processes and determine which method will make the best sense for you.

Chapter 2: Certification With The Six Sigma Black Belt And Achieving Success

Achieving the Black Belt in the Six Sigma program is going to mean earning all the necessary achievements to reach that level. These achievements are going to vary from company to company. Those who take a course through a school or other type of education entity will find that they must first complete their Green Belt schooling in order to move onto obtaining their Black Belt. There are some companies who set forth their own Six Sigma program, and they will have their own learning aspects that must be met. If this is the case for you, then you must talk with your company about what is going to be required in order to achieve this level.

Those who are looking at an education entity to provide this coursework are going to find that the Green Belt most often means completing two weeks of training, and then passing a qualification exam at the end. This is the basic course that is going to teach the fundamentals and methodologies of the Six Sigma program. Once this level has been reached, a person can then advance onto earning their Black Belt.

The Black Belt program is given to those who complete their Green Belt, then complete four additional weeks of training. One of the interesting aspects about this belt is that most often, those who have achieved their Black Belt are going to be teaching those who are aspiring to the Green Belt. It is believed that through teaching the methodologies and showcasing them in real life, a person will learn how to implement them better on their own.For those who do go with a third-party education facility, they will often receive some sort of certification documentation that they can use in other places of employment, rather than just in their current employment. Therefore, becoming a Six Sigma Black Belt is something that business professionals can do on their own, even if the current business they work for is not interested in this type of information. It is just one way in which a business professional can put themselves into the market with more credentials than those who they are competing against.

Expectations of Six Sigma Black Belt Holders

Those who are becoming certified with Six Sigma as a Black Belt are going to find that there are several expectations demanded of them in order to earn it. Of course, these expectations are going to differ depending upon what teacher the person has. However, here are just a few examples of what a person will have to know in order to pass the final exam:

Be able to explain the methodologies of Six Sigma, as well as the principles, tools and measurements that are used alongside them.

Understand leadership and responsibility, while also being able to effectively showcase that they have the ability to utilize these skills.

Be able to understand the financials of a business and the ways in which these can be measured.

Understand time management and planning, along with other team managing techniques, and be able to implement them.

Understand what a project charter is and how to define it.

Understand the purpose of customer feedback and how to put it to use effectively when working on problems.

Understand control plans and how to develop them for business implementation.

Be able to use various types of measurement tools, including:

Hypothesis testing

Results analysis

Complete measurement systems

Cause analysis tools

Gap analysis tools

Be able to recognize waste in the business and know methods for reducing it.

Finding Success with the Six Sigma Black Belt Program

No one should enter into the Black Belt program if they are not ready to do the work. These are course-intensive programs that will rely on the person's knowledge of business and build upon what they already know. In order to find success with this program, those who have been through this and have achieved certification have several tidbits for advice:

The best method for learning these methodologies is to put them into practice on your own. Learning from someone is going to help you accomplish this. Through being more hands on with this type of program, the concepts are going to stick in your mind much better than simply through reading about this coursework.

Only start on this program when you know you have the time to devote to learning the concepts. Without devoting the time, you cannot predict success with this program.

Though this type of certification is going to be beneficial to all business professionals, you must truly decide that you are ready to undergo this type of commitment and that this is the right belt for you. Full dedication is needed; otherwise, you will not reap the benefits that this belt has to offer.

Study hard and study often in order to make sure that these concepts are sticking in your mind.

Consider utilizing mock situations in order to put these practices to use in order to gain the full meaning behind the methodologies.

Though many may consider the Six Sigma Black Belt course difficult, you can still succeed. The key is to be ready for what lies ahead and ensure that you are devoting your attention to it.

Chapter 3: Introduction To Lean Six Sigma

The Six Sigma strategies aim to achieve, sustain, and maximize success in business. A system tries to understand fully customer requirements by looking into data, facts, and statistical analysis to manage, improve, and reinvent processes diligently. It reduces process variation using statistical tools in order to achieve defect-free products and services.

The Five Stages of Six Sigma Methodologies

Projects involving Six Sigma follow the DMAIC framework, which means Define, Measure, Analyze, Improve, and Control. Every phase has its own techniques and tools that help the business improve processes from beginning to end.

What is Lean Six Sigma?

Lean Speed or Lean Method is a collection of tools used for reducing waste produced by the flow of information and materials. The primary objective of Lean is to determine and get rid of non-value-added and non-essential steps of the business process in order to streamline production; gain customer loyalty; and improve quality.

Lean Methods used within the DMAIC framework can support the tools of Six Sigma that improve efficiency and speed of the business process. Consultants in Six Sigma and Lean Methods realized the synergy of the two strategies in the 1980s. They combined the various tools in order to improve quality and remove waste. With the combined techniques, organizations can solve different business problems.

Lean Six Sigma boosts the strengths and reduces the weaknesses of each of the strategies. It emphasizes the use of tools and methodologies to determine and get rid of waste, and maximize process speed. Furthermore, it identifies and minimizes or eliminates process variation.

What is a Lean Six Sigma Belt?

A belt corresponds to the experience level of a Lean Six Sigma practitioner. Like in martial arts, the darker the color of the belt, the more experienced a practitioner is.

Black Belt

A black belt practitioner is someone who has experience and expertise in the DMAIC (Define, Measure, Analyze, Improve, and Control) methodology, team leadership, and Lean strategies. He can lead any team within the corporation in executing the various projects of Lean Six Sigma. He can also conduct training, coach, and mentor other employees in Lean Six Sigma.

A person can achieve the black belt by attending training for it. The course is usually 140 to 160 hours long. It includes the project management and team leadership, as well as designed experiments and statistical data analysis.

Green Belt

A green belt practitioner exhibits strong skills and knowledge in Lean methods and DMAIC methodology. However, he has no experience with advanced statistical tools. He may lead simple projects or work as a team member. If he is to lead projects, a black belt practitioner must supervise him. A green belt trading lasts for at most 100 hours and includes problem-solving techniques and simple statistical data analysis.

Yellow Belt

A yellow belt practitioner knows basic tools and general concepts of Lean Six Sigma. He can be a team member after completion of training. He can be responsible for data gathering for a black belt or green belt project.

The yellow belt training can differ, depending on the organization. He may learn the DMAIC process with the basic language and concepts of Six Sigma. He may also complete the training that last between 15 to 25 hours.

Champion

A champion is a high-ranking manager who works with a black belt practitioner. His main task is to ensure project success by removing barriers. He also ensures that the project has organizational support. A champion is not necessarily an expert. He has organizational knowledge and helps the project align with the strategic objectives of the company.

White Belt

A white belt practitioner has awareness training. He is either a staff or executive who assist cultural buy-in and change management from professional who do not use the tools. A Lean Six Sigma project may affect him so he needs to learn about the basics of improving processes.

Design for Six Sigma

The Design for Six Sigma is another methodology that designs a process or product to meet the requirements of the customer. Instead of improving the product or process later, it aims to get the process or product right the first time. The Design for Lean Six Sigma, on the other hand, is a combination of all techniques and tools.

Six Sigma versus Lean Six Sigma

Six Sigma's goal is to improve efficiency and quality by eliminating waste and defects. It improves and streamlines business processes. Although used primarily in manufacturing, Six Sigma practitioners are now in various industries and fields. They achieve measurable and real results that help their companies.

The Lean approach, on the hand, emphasizes eliminating wasteful and unnecessary steps in product creation in order to streamline production and manufacturing processes. It propagates the use of essential steps that add value to the product directly.

In essence, both strategies have the same objective. They both search for ways to get rid of waste in order to make the system as efficient as possible. However, Six Sigma and Lean methodologies differ in their approaches on how to achieve their goal. Simply put, they differ in identifying the root cause of waste.

Lean practitioners identify waste as an unnecessary step in the production process. They believe that waste does not add value to the product. On the other hand, Six Sigma practitioners determine waste as a process variation. Both of their assessments are true thus, both of them are successful in improving performance of the business. However, they are most successful when combined.

Chapter 4: Implementing Six Sigma

No two organizations are exactly alike. They may exist within the same market or industry, but they face different sets of challenges. Therefore, the strategies that they use when implementing Six Sigma will vary significantly, especially if you consider their organizational culture and strategic goals.

In this chapter, you will learn how Six Sigma can be implemented within an organization and how to get top management to commit and support it. You will also learn how to reduce lead time to improve customer satisfaction and ensure business success.

There are generally two approaches that an organization can use when implementing Six Sigma:

• Execute a Six Sigma initiative or program

• Establish a Six Sigma infrastructure

Executing a Six Sigma Initiative or Program

This option involves training specific employees on how to apply Six Sigma tools in the workplace. It is an unstructured way of implementing Six Sigma in an organization. A few practitioners are chosen and trained on how to use statistical tools whenever they feel that it is necessary to apply the tool. If the Six Sigma practitioners get stuck, they can ask a statistician for help.

Though this approach may yield some successes within the company, these are few and far between.

The simple reason is that there is not enough consistency, and therefore, each success fails to provide the support for the next one. It is as if there is a lack of total commitment to fully implement the Six Sigma methodology throughout the organization.

An organization that focuses on implementing Six Sigma as a mere program will only change a few of their tools and introduce a couple of training classes for the affected employees. If it were to go further, it might apply these tools to a number of special projects.

However, these projects are rarely a core part of the organization. These projects tend to be low-level initiatives that have not even been endorsed by top management. If the solution that the project is meant to provide directly affects upper management, then it is possible that the project will experience a lot of internal resistance.

It is clear to see that implementing Six Sigma through tools alone is not likely to boost the bottom line or add value to the long-term, strategic goals of the organization. This approach usually leads to Six Sigma being viewed as a fashionable methodology that is only useful during certain seasons. There will be a minimal return on the investment made to train employees.

No matter what kind of extraordinary achievements are made through the use of Six Sigma tools, the benefits will not be visible to top management.

Their resistance to Six Sigma ultimately kills any attempts to bring change, and with no assigned change champion, even getting funds to finance the initiative becomes tough. Ultimately, success can only be achieved by convincing upper management to support Six Sigma implementation throughout the organization.

Establishing a Six Sigma Infrastructure

The best way to implement Six Sigma in an organization is to focus on establishing a solid infrastructure that will guide all Six Sigma projects. This goes way beyond just introducing a couple of statistical tools that are used haphazardly.

This particular option focuses on gaining top management buy-in before any investment in Six Sigma is made.

Employees are trained to use the right tools at the right time when working on a predefined project.

Six Sigma practitioners are selected and trained for a period of four months, and in between training sessions, they are given projects to help them apply what they have learned.

An organization that invests time and money to deploy Six Sigma as part of its broader business strategy will benefit more than the one that simply deploys Six Sigma tools. Here are some of the benefits of deploying Six Sigma infrastructure with the support of upper management:

● The projects deployed directly affect the bottom line, thus achieving a bigger impact

● Six Sigma tools are used more effectively, efficiently, and productively

- It provides a project management strategy that practitioners can study and improve upon

- It makes it easier for the practitioners and upper management to communicate

- Critical business processes can be understood in detail

- It helps managers and employees understand the real value of statistical tools to the organization

One of the key steps in deploying a Six Sigma project is the project selection process. It is important to select projects that will help the organization meet its strategic business goals. Six Sigma can be a useful and effective roadmap for achieving these goals.

Regardless of how an organization chooses to implement Six Sigma, the important thing to note is that Six Sigma should be a long-term commitment. This will ensure that there is an objective analysis of every element in the business process.

It will be easier to learn from past mistakes and improve on subsequent implementation plans. This will create a closed feedback loop that ultimately reaps dividends for the organization.

Overcoming Upper Management Reluctance

There are certain measures that you can take to overcome top management resistance to Six Sigma. Here are five steps to take to gain management support:

Choose your projects wisely – If you develop the right project selection criteria, you stand a better chance of picking projects that will have the greatest impact on the company's bottom line. This will prove to top management that Six Sigma is of value.

Get quick results – Make sure that the project bears fast results and generates significant returns. You will have about five weeks to show management that you can reduce costs and improve productivity by at least 30 percent.

Track your interim progress – Develop a work plan that specifies key milestones, responsibilities, and deliverables.

Gather an expert team – You may have to seek Six Sigma experts from within or outside the organization as part of your deployment team. Having qualified professionals increases the chances of project success. This will convince top management to consider implementing Six Sigma throughout the entire organization.

Maintain a clearly defined project scope – Make sure that the project scope is wide enough to generate significant returns but also narrow enough to enable quick completion.

Once top management sees the practical benefits of Six Sigma, they may consider a limited initial commitment or a broad-based rollout of Six Sigma throughout the organization.

Lead Time

Lead time is defined as the time from which the customer places an order to the moment the product or service is delivered. Every type of business has some form of lead time, whether it is in manufacturing, project management, software development, supply chain management, etc. The only difference is how lead time is interpreted in that particular industry.

But why is lead time so important in business?

Because time is money!

Let's say that a manufacturer usually buys steel from a supplier. Imagine a situation where the supplier has a lead time of one month. This means that the supplier takes one month to deliver an order for steel to the manufacturer. Therefore, the manufacturer needs to maintain an inventory of one month's worth of steel to keep producing products for their customers.

Maintaining inventory means paying storage costs for the steel, so the longer the supplier's lead time, the greater the storage charges. It would be in the manufacturer's best interest to find a supplier who can supply the steel within a shorter period of time.

A longer lead time is also disadvantageous because it forces the manufacturer to be more precise with their demand forecast. If customer demand exceeds the forecast, delivery of products to the customers will be delayed. This will cause customer dissatisfaction. This is why reducing lead time is very important in business.

Components of lead time

Lead time consists of several different elements that originate from the various departments within an organization. These include:

- Preprocessing time — This is the time it takes to receive an order from the customer, understand the order, and then create a purchase order.

- Waiting time — The time an item has to spend awaiting production

- Processing time — The time it takes to produce an item

- Inspection time — The time it takes to check a product for conformity tostandards

- Storage time — The amount of time an item stays in the factory or warehouse

- Transportation time — The amount of time the product is in transit from the factory to the customer

When you add up all these elements, you end up with the total lead time. One assumption that is made is that there is no inventory in storage. In other words, we assume that the product must be made from scratch.

So the challenge you have is to find a way to reduce the lead time.

How to reduce lead time

Eliminate non-value activities – Use value stream mapping to find those activities that do not add value to the process and eliminate them.

Simplify the production process – When you make the process less complex, production flows faster.

Improve layout – Arrange the machinery and work process such that raw materials and finished goods do not have to move long distances.

Document your operating procedure – Create a document for standard operating procedures so that every employee is familiar with what is required. This will enable quick learning, less confusion, and enhanced consistency.

Planned machinery maintenance – It is better to schedule the regular maintenance of machinery than to wait for a total shutdown that will cripple production.

Find backup suppliers — Create an arrangement with a group of suppliers so that in case one supplier lets you down, you can rely on another. Take time to educate your suppliers on how your operations are run so that they understand how important they are in your business process.

The truth is that customers will always gravitate toward companies that have shorter lead times. Any organization that works to reduce its lead time will ultimately improve its chances of success.

In the next chapter, you will learn the steps necessary to apply the DMAIC framework.

Chapter 5: The Steps To Lean Six Sigma Implementations

Once the higher tier management has taken the decision to benefit from lean six sigma, they can follow the eight steps below. You will be able to develop an infrastructure for adopting all the new techniques for enhancing cohesion between the workforce.

Step 1: Create a Burning Platform:

Your company must have a strong issue which forced you to implement the program. Knowing this issue is important because you will be able to hear the efforts in that department then. Reasons can be anything from quality losses to falling out of the race with competitors. Without this burning platform, people won't be able to muster the motivation to work on the lean six sigma.

Step 2: Put Resources in Place

By resources, we mean appointing the professionals with sigma certification. If your company needs a yellow belt or a black belt, hire accordingly. And make sure this person that you appoint understands your reason for six sigma implementation and is able to cohesively work with your team. Don't hold back in employees, material, technology, equipment, and more.

Every resource that you get should play an important role. And getting all these resources in one place is not the only thing you need to do, you also need to make sure that they are all coherent and woke together as a team. They must be motivated and dedicated enough to carry out the initiatives set by the six sigma policy.

Step 3: Teach the Methodology

After deciding on what steps of which recessed you are targeting with six sigma, make sure you belt out these steps and there expected improvements with your employee and everyone else involved so that they too should know your final goal. Aware of the entire organization.

At the same time, maintain the energy in your workforce and motivate them to become agents of change. Train members of your workforce to attain either a yellow belt, green belt, or black belt and hire a professional long with this to increase the effectiveness of your sigma tools. The employees being trained, the professional hired, and the organization heads should all be on the same page.

Step 4: Prioritize Activities

Once you have the required resources and your employees are being trained in the important sectors and areas of concern, opportunities start to present themselves. At this point, the main objective of the organization should be to listen to the customer.

This way, they can filter out what they require, and that is identifying the CTQs of the critical to quality criteria. Now you need to develop metrics in order to know which activity renders which improvement in which sector.

This is basically ensuring that every lean six sigma effort is leading to a business goal and is helping you eradicate your initial worry for the deployment of lean six sigma in your organization. You should know when to take risks and when to overlook the shortcomings. Activities should be assessed on a daily basis.

Step 5: Establish Ownership

Ownership helps you to appoint one person in charge of looking over the implementation of the six sigma policy. This person rings together with the workforce and directs them to a single cause. This person is responsible for keeping the spirits high, and everyone motivated. He is responsible for making sure all assigned activities are meeting with the initial goal. This way, you know who to hold accountable for and who to inquire from about the progress of the system. You can appoint a committee or a person that's up to you.

Step 6: Take the right Measurements

Every objective that you have needs to be met with activities taking place under the banner of six sigma. So how do you ensure that all your activities are resulting in improving your defects and resulting in operational efficiencies? For that, you take into consideration some measurements and metrics.

If there is something that cannot be measured, it cannot be improved. You are able to measure the duration of a delivery process, so you can work towards improving it. You cannot measure factors like the weather on the day of delivery, so you cannot work to improve that.

When measurement systems are made in accordance with the six sigma tools, professionals are able to devise a baseline or standard performance and then use the data obtained from different activities objective decision making and limiting variation. Make sure that the metrics and indicators that you set are actually true measurements of what goal you are trying to achieve. These indicators should not be lagging and should not be too many that you get misled.

The key to effective measurement is able to get the cost of the quality right. At the same time, efforts must be made to get these measurements faster. You have the unit to measure, but the data should come in faster too. So decisions via analysis can be made faster.

Step 7: Govern the lean six sigma program:

Setting up a governing body helps to maintain the momentum and helps to perpetuate the initial goal. Poor governance makes the workforce unmotivated and divided too. They don't have a single cause to woe towards a, and there's no one to hold them accountable for their inefficient working procedures.

At the same time, too much governance can also hurt the system by making the vision fall apart. To make sure your governance is powering through, hold daily meetings, and schedule a daily overview of the process implementation to fix any nonessential activities quickly. Highlight common challenges in departments and exchange words of motivation so that everyone can stay on track.

Step 8: Recognition of Contributions:

This step is often looked over but is extremely significant. Rewarding and acknowledging the efforts of a few hardworking individuals does not only motivate them to strive harder but also makes them a role model for others to follow, who then also start working harder in order to receive appreciation and acknowledgment. It uplifts the spirits of everyone from the bottom to the top and even freshens up the brains of people, giving them a little relaxation. This can act positively as his light gives them a break to do something innovative and come into with more zeal and zest the next time. So always look towards rewarding employees and celebrating the littlest of victories and improvements.

A positive attitude helps people to grow and develop. It creates a productive atmosphere where everyone feels a part of a system and feels like they are valued. When they notice their name associated with the company, it makes them work even harder because now it's their name on the line too.

All these steps to implementation of the lean six sigma theory are extremely important. Skipping one can make you lag and put you behind your competitors.

Chapter 6: The Difference Between Lean And Lean Six Sigma

As mentioned before, understanding Lean thinking is crucial to understanding Lean Six Sigma and where it falls in the agile spectrum. At the same time, however, it is quite important that you take your time to learn how Lean and Six Sigma correlate with each other, both in terms of differences and in terms of characteristics that are common (or similar) to both approaches.

This chapter is dedicated to helping you gain a better understanding of what these similarities and differences are so that you can further apply the Lean Six Sigma method in your projects.

Differences between Lean and Six Sigma

Although somewhat pertaining to the same spectrum, Lean and Six Sigma pose significant differences you should be fully aware of when applying either of them (or their offspring, Lean Six Sigma) to your project management methodologies and process.

Perhaps the single most important difference between Lean and Six Sigma is consisted of the main issue they aim to solve. While Lean centers its focus on waste, Six Sigma centers it on variation (or, better said, on avoiding variation).

Furthermore, the techniques employed by the two methods are different as well. Lean management relies on visual techniques to analyze situations and processes, as well as to create solutions (which are normally supported by data analysis). Six Sigma, on the other hand, uses statistical techniques to analyze processes and create solutions, and they are all supported by data visualization.

Many people believe Lean is easier to learn (and apply) than Six Sigma is. The misconception is mostly connected to the fact that Lean visuals are easier to understand, while Six Sigma's mostly numerical analysis is difficult. However, this is not entirely true. While the misconception may have been closer to reality back in the day, today's statistical support tools make both approaches equally easy to understand and employ.

Last, but not least, another major difference between Lean and Six Sigma consists of the documentation types used for the solution that was found. Lean thinking uses a revised value stream mapping system to generate the needed changes in the workflow. At the same time, Six Sigma is documented using changes that have been applied in the setup procedures, as well as the control plan employed to monitor the process and respond to any kind of variation. As a consequence, this type of documentation will change work instructions, as well as the measurement approach and the systems used in a given process.

Similarities between Lean and Six Sigma

If you look at the aforementioned comparison only, you would be tempted to think that reconciliation between Lean and Six Sigma is difficult - and then, you would wonder how on Earth did Lean Six Sigma even manage to exist.

Beyond all the differences mentioned above, however, Lean and Six Sigma are very similar in nature - and it all starts with the fact that both of them place the customer experience at the center of everything they do.

Moreover, both Lean and Six Sigma use a special type of flow mapping approach that helps project managers and team members to understand the process. Regardless of whether the analysis is based on a product or service, both Lean and Six Sigma will always use some sort of process to associate with the creation and delivery of that product or service.

Furthermore, both Lean and Six Sigma are heavily reliant on data, which helps managers determine the current performance and how future performance could be impacted.

Another similarity between the two approaches is consisted of the fact that they are both used as improvement methods - and the changes will usually be implemented by cross-functional teams.

As a natural consequence of the main focus behind Lean and Six Sigma, both of them will reduce waste and variation in processes. Waste and variation are tightly connected, as removing wasted steps will eliminate the variations, while removing variation can help eliminate waste.

Last, but definitely not least, the evolution of the two project management methods analyzed here is similar as well. While they might have started in manufacturing operation, both Lean and Six Sigma are now used on all functions of a company, across a variety of industries. If a business relies on processes to create its products and services and bring them to market,

Lean, Six Sigma, and Lean Six Sigma will prove to be more than useful.

Chapter 7: Understanding Value

The first step in using the 5S methodologies to create a leaner enterprise is to understand the value of the goods or the services you are selling. Why should a customer use your company to fulfill their needs? In order to answer that question, you need to examine what it is that you provide, and identify what it is worth, both to you and to the consumer. When you can say that you have a deep understanding of that worth, you'll have identified the **value** of your product. For some perspective, let's first take a look at value from a consumer's point of view,

When you are going to make a purchase, large or small, you look at the price tag, which gives you the dollar value of that good or service. Have you ever stopped to think about how and why the price is determined to be what it is? There are raw materials, labor, and shipping or transportation costs associated with every single thing that is purchased or every service that is performed every day. It's the culmination of those factors that results in the asking price- so how do you determine the product's actual value?

Let's say you want to purchase a used car for your teenager to use as their first vehicle. Think about the factors that will play into your decision. You'll want to consider what price you are willing to pay for that vehicle, but that's not the only thing you should base your decision on. You'll want to look for a vehicle that still has quality, one that won't break down regularly and need expensive repairs- that's a waste of money you could have spent on just buying a higher-quality vehicle to begin with, not to mention the burden and frustration of constant vehicle issues. Added to that is the possibility that the car may become irreparable, sending you back to square one down the money you'd spent on the first one plus repairs.

You'll also want to consider safety, for your own peace of mind, as well as how safety affects secondary costs such as insurance. There's a direct correlation between insurance rates and vehicle safety, so you can find more value for your money by purchasing a vehicle with better safety features such as airbags and antilock braking systems. Another factor in your decision will understandably be aesthetics. Is your teenager going to want to drive a car with unsightly dents or one that's crying out for a paint job? The need to put money into cosmetic work is another thing that detracts from the vehicle's overall value.

As you've figured out by now, value is not defined by one single factor, but rather a culmination of factors coming together to determine the overall value of a product. The same goes for services; you would never want to pay for a cheap plumber who doesn't have the skillset or tools needed to properly repair your water issues, requiring several visits over time. It's a much greater value to pay a higher price point for a plumber who can fix the problem in one visit and be done with it.

As a business owner, it's important to be able to see value from your customers' point of view. When you can do that, you are better equipped to understand the value of your business process and your finished product. To your customer, value begins the moment they first contact you, but to your business, value has to begin before that, with quality tools to perform your services and quality raw materials to produce your goods.

If you own a towing company, where you source your tow trucks and flatbeds from, it can make all the difference in your efficiency and your ability to perform your advertised service. To the customer, your value is in your capability to quickly and safely get their vehicle off the side of the road. To you, the value lies in knowing that your trucks are reliable and safe for your employees. The value must begin with you and be passed onto the consumer.

To give another example of value, let's say you own a bakery and must produce dozens of cookies, cupcakes, and muffins every day. One of your biggest raw material purchases is going to be flour, which can vary vastly in quality and price. If you purchase flour that isn't of the highest quality, the product which you present to the public will suffer. Now, let's say you use the low-quality flour and sell your cupcakes at a price point that would be better suited to high-quality flour. Your customers will recognize that you're not charging a fair price; they will no longer think that your products are worth the cost because they will not feel that they are getting value for their money.

The lesson to be learned from the bakery example is to price your finished product commensurate with the costs of your raw materials. No one likes price gouging, and while you are trying to save money, you MUST balance that with the need to retain customers. This is one of the hardest parts of understanding value. Value is never only defined by a price tag. Examine your finished product, examine your raw materials, and take the time to make lists of what is vital for the quality manufacture of your goods or the exemplary performance of your services. Consider things like:

Time to receive raw materials

Cost and quality of raw materials

Cost of labor

Customer needs and wants

Longevity of product/frequency of service

Changing and expanding customer bases

If you own a business that most consumers only need once in a while, you can afford to have a large customer base, because you'll be able to provide quality services to those clients if and when they need you. If you provide a service that people need more frequently, you may keep a smaller customer base to ensure quality, or you may choose to hire more employees and expand your clientele. You can choose which factors to manipulate because there are certain fixed elements which you cannot work around, such as the time it takes for certain tasks to be completed. A job which takes an hour will always take an hour, no matter how skilled your employees are. The one thing you can never sacrifice is the value of your goods or services.

Now that we've taken a long look at how we define value in lean enterprise, you can see why it's so important to every industry. Value is what keeps customers coming back to your business. If you can identify and understand the value within all your products and services, you'll be well on your way to building a leaner enterprise in no time.

Once you've identified what value means to you, it will be much easier to complete the next step: Following Value. This means being able to identify the value of every step of your business process. This allows you to evaluate areas that need improvement and areas where you're doing well. If you're ready, let's head on over to Chapter 3, where we'll be explaining how you can examine and increase the value of your business practices from start to end.

Chapter 8: Lean 5s

When it comes to determining what wasteful processes you are dealing with, it is important to ensure the work environment is in optimum shape for the best results. The 5S organizational methodology is one commonly used system based around a number of Japanese words that, when taken together, are first-rate when it comes to improving efficiency and effectiveness by clearly identifying and storing items in their designated space each and every time.

The goal here is to allow for standardization across a variety of processes which will ultimately generate significant time savings in the long-term. The reason it is so effective is that each time the human eye tracks across a messy workspace, it takes a fraction of a second to locate what it is looking for and process everything around it. While this might not be much if it happens now and then, if it is happening constantly across an entire team, then it can add up to serious time loss when taken across the sum total of the process in question

Sorting: Sorting is all about doing what can be done in order to always keep the workplace clean of anything that isn't required. When sorting, it is important to organize the space in such a way that it removes anything that would create an obstacle towards the completion of the task at hand. You will want to ensure that process-critical items all have a unique space that is labeled as well as a space that is designated for those things that simply don't fit anywhere else. Moving forward, this will make it easier to keep the space free of new distractions. Nevertheless, it will still be important to encourage team members to prune their personal space regularly to keep new obstacles from popping up.

Set in order: When it comes to organizing the items in the workspace themselves, it is important to ensure all the items are organized in the order that they will most likely be used. While doing so, it is important to take care to ensure that everything required for the most common steps remains readily at hand to reduce movement waste as much as possible. Over time, keeping things in the same place will ensure that the process can be completed faster each time as muscle memory takes over, and team members are able to reach for things without looking for them.

It is important to keep an open mind during this step since ensuring that the workspace is set up in such a way that ease of workflow is promoted may require more than a simple organization, it may require a serious rework of existing facilities. Additionally, ensuring everything is arranged correctly will make it easier for you to create steps for each part of the process that anyone new to that part of the process can follow.

Shine: Keeping the workspace clean is an essential part of maintaining the most effective workspace possible. It is important to emphasize the importance of daily cleaning both for the overall efficiency boost and its ability to ensure that everything is where it is supposed to be so that there are no issues the next time they are needed. This will also provide an opportunity to have regular maintenance if any is needed, which will serve to make the office a safer place for everyone. The end goal should be that any member of the team should be able to enter a new space and understand where the key items are located in less than five minutes.

Standardize: The standardize step is all about making sure the organizational process itself is organized in such a way that it can be applied throughout the entire business structure. This will make it easier to maintain order when things get hectic and also ensure that everyone can be held to the same reliable standard.

Sustain: Sustaining the process is vital as taking a week or more to properly get everything in order only to have it all fall apart six months later is going to accomplish nothing in the long-term. As such, it is important to ensure that the organization is a vital part of the DNA of the business in moving forward. If things are truly sustainable in this regard, then team members will be able to successfully move through the process without expressly being asked to. Unfortunately, you won't be able to expect this type of sustainability overnight. It will require plenty of training and adoption of the idea as part of the business's culture.

Great starter tool: If your plan for your business is to transition to additional advanced Lean concepts over time, then 5S is a great way to start moving employees in that direction. It is especially effective with employees who are extremely stuck in their ways as, once they initially get on board, they will be hard-pressed to deny the benefits in completion times that come with the improved organizational version. This, in turn, will make it easier for them to get on board with additional changes that may come in the future.

As a rule, when rolling out a new system like this, you can expect team members to only care about two things, the way the new system is going to affect them specifically and if the Lean process has actually seen results. This is also what makes 5S a great starting point as it has easily understandable answers for each that anyone can understand once they see the first workspace transformed for efficiency.

Knowing if 5S is right for your business:While 5S is a great choice for some businesses, it is not a one-size-fits-all solution, which means it is important to understand both of its strengths and its weaknesses when moving forward. Perhaps its biggest strength is that when implemented successfully, it is sure to help your team define their processes more easily while also helping them claim more ownership of the processes they are associated with as well. This extra structure also has the potential to lead to a much greater degree of personal responsibility among team members which will lead to a greater feeling of accountability throughout the process. When everything goes according to plan, this will then lead to further improved performance and better working conditions for everyone involved.

What's more, implementing 5S also has the potential to more likely make long-term employee contributions thanks to an internalized sense of improvement. Ideally, this will continue until the idea of continuous improvement becomes the order of the day. When done correctly, using 5S will also provide further insight into the realm of value analysis, equipment reliability, and work standardization.

On the other hand, the biggest weakness of 5S is that if it, and its purpose, are not communicated properly, then team members can make the mistake of seeing it as the end goal and not a means to an end. 5S should be the flagbearer for success to come in the future, not the sum total of a company's journey into Lean processes. Specifically, businesses whose movement is constrained significantly by external factors will have a hard time using 5S, and companies that currently have a storage problem would do well to solve it before attempting a 5S transition.

Additionally, just because 5S is a great fit for many companies doesn't mean that it will be the best choice for your team. This is especially true for smaller teams or for teams where team members wear many hats. Just because it is a popular way to implement Lean principles doesn't mean that it is going to be right for everyone. Moving ahead anyway and enforcing organization simply for the sake of organization won't do much of anything when it comes to generating real results. Instead, it will only generate new waste and it will only continue to do so before it is abandoned entirely.

This is especially true for businesses that run on a wide variety of human interaction, various management styles, and other management tools. However, when the various aspects work together properly, they will actually end up generating extra value for the customer which is a vital part of any successful business. If you blindly press forward with a 5S mentality, however, then it can become easy to lose sight of the outcome for the customer in pursuit of a perfect outcome or a perfect implementation of 5S principles.

Above all else, when implementing 5S, it is important that you stress to your team that 5S is something that should be part of the natural work routine and standard best practices, not an additional task to be done outside of daily work. The goal of 5S is to enhance the effectiveness of the workflow at every step in the process. Separating out the 5S into its own separate layer is the complete opposite of what the process stands for.

Chapter 9: Six Sigma Certification The Importance

There is not a company in this world who would not be familiar with Six sigma Training.

Any company that dreams about getting famous, rich and wealthy not only knows about Six sigma method and six sigma courses but also tries to implement these courses in their projects.

SIGMA METHOD?

Six Sigma is the method that is used for finding out the factors that help in lowering the quality of the output. The method finds those factors and then eradicates them completely thus improving the efficiency and the effectiveness of the product.

Companies crave for employees with six sigma certification. If a person gets six sigma training then they get a certificate that becomes the proof that the person has been trained in six sigma courses.

The six sigma certification works like a golden ticket for employees that need jobs in big firms.

Many companies offer six sigma courses within their organizations. This is a benefit for the employees who want to have six sigma certification. However, there are many companies that cannot offer the training course on this method. In this case, the employees of these companies have to get trained in this method on their own.

Whatever the scenario is, employees with six sigma certification can either look for better options or get promotions and bonuses in their companies.

FOUR LEVELS OF THE COURSE:

The course involves four levels and the employees can either get training in all of them or anyone of them or whatever suits them. There are Yellow belts, Green belts, Black belts and Champions.

Employees with Yellow belts six sigma certification are the beginners. They get all the required training but still they are not trained enough to be given independent projects. Independent projects are the ones in which the person acts as the head or the manager of the project.

Employees with Six Sigma Green Belt certification are the most-wanted ones by the industries because they are the ones that are given the practical training and also some knowledge about the DMAIC (Define Measure Analyze Improve Control) Method.

They are given extensive six sigma green belt training courses to improve their knowledge.

Employees with six sigma black belt certification or with Champion certification are the ones that help the

Yellow Belts and Green Belts. These are given six sigma black belt training courses.

Black Belts ensure that proper six sigma methods are being used in the processes while Champions are the heads of the projects that monitor the overall process.

WHAT IS THE ADVANTAGE OF HAVING SIX SIGMA CERTIFICATION?

The advantage of Six sigma certification is that a person becomes capable of debugging the errors of his project. A project's output is not of any success if it is not what the client aspires of. The method helps in removing the errors and maintaining the quality of the product.

This results in increasing the sales of the company, its market value, customers' trust in that company and their satisfaction. If a client gets what he wants then he is definitely going to approach that company the next time too when he has a project.

SIX SIGMA; WAY TO DEVELOP PEOPLE

One of the many benefits of Six Sigma is how it helps to develop people. The dual processes of Six Sigma training and Six Sigma projects cultivate excellence in not only product quality and financial savings but also in the knowledge, confidence, and quality of the people in your organization. People are, after all, your organizations' most valuable assets.

To sustain and continuously improve, an organization needs to develop its people. Six Sigma helps to develop your people in two areas: it develops leaders and it empowers people to be knowledgeable and valuable contributors to the organization's success.

Every organization needs people with leadership qualities. Leadership skills are needed at every level in the organization. Consistent Six Sigma training and implementation from the executive level through line managers will help grow leadership in your organization.

With Six Sigma, there are many opportunities to develop leadership skills and leadership qualities at all levels in the organization. Six Sigma certification training and the hands-on real-world training of leading Six Sigma projects cultivate management skills.

Six Sigma seeks to grow leaders in an organization through its training programs. People who have completed Six Sigma training earn a Belt title. It denotes their level of knowledge and responsibility.

A Green Belt is an individual who has completed two weeks of training on the Six Sigma roadmap and essential elements of statistical methodologies supporting Six Sigma projects and who is a member of a Six Sigma process improvement team. A Black Belt is an individual who has completed four weeks of training focusing on the Six Sigma Roadmap and extensive statistical methodologies and is experienced in leading cross-functional process improvement teams.

Black Belts become leaders of Six Sigma project teams and they mentor other employees to help them improve. Six Sigma values leadership, but it also values involvement from employees at all levels of the organization. If anyone can get to the root of a problem and help solve it, then it doesn't matter where the idea comes from.

Six Sigma has to have complete support and commitment from all levels of the organization. Six Sigma requires buy-in from everyone involved in the business processes that are measured. This requirement actually helps build a better organization.

Involvement from all levels of employees comes about from the Six Sigma strategy of building project teams. Continuous improvement processes, such as Six Sigma, means including people, gaining their involvement, and then supporting what they are trying to accomplish.

Six Sigma asks for input on improvement solutions from all employees because it recognizes the value of creative solutions to problems from any and all sources. The simple reality is that line workers know some things the higher ups don't. Front-line employees understand the customer better than anyone. Organizations that solicit ideas from line workers will uncover innovative solutions to problems that could never be uncovered by detached analysis.

Involving people through Six Sigma also leads to empowering people. Six Sigma's data-driven methodology gives people appropriate feedback on the process and levels of improvement they are achieving-what they did well and what they did badly.

Through Six Sigma, your people are given real solutions to eliminate the real root causes of problems. Plus, it gives them the understanding of the what's, where's, and why's because the data is there. Thus, Six Sigma helps to develop the knowledge, confidence, and quality of the people in your organization.

Further, Six Sigma helps promote a culture of trust so that everyone's energies will be directed into positive and constructive work. Such a culture consists of including people, giving them the tools they need to succeed, an appropriate level of influence and control, and being open with them.

As trust builds people start to get more involved, become more committed, accept more empowerment, and deeper levels of trust develop. Team work, coordination of activities, trust amongst the team, and knowing the process makes the effort of Six Sigma successful.

The result of doing this well is professional growth, improved morale and positive attitudes toward cooperative efforts. Six Sigma will become one of the factors that not only fuels dramatic quality improvement in your employees but create an outstanding workplace.

SIX SIGMA KEY ELEMENTS

Six Sigma is basically an enterprise procedure that allows businesses to boost their profit margins. Six Sigma stands for Six Normal Deviations.

Six Sigma methodology supplies the methods and instruments to increase the capability and reduce the flaws in any procedure. (Sigma would be the Greek letter utilized to symbolize regular deviation in statistics) from necessarily mean.

Six Sigma is often a structured and disciplined, data-driven approach for enhancing business. It focuses on how we will boost our competitiveness inside marketplace by increasing consumer satisfaction, enhancing worker involvement, instilling optimistic change into our way of life and in the long run making bottom and best line growth.

In the highest level, Six Sigma is all about satisfying buyer wants profitably. It really is a highly disciplined methodology that assists create and successfully supply near-perfect products and services.

Six Sigma has proved alone by showing results planet broad and by generating substantial enterprise returns. Six Sigma has turn out to be vital for all organization and companies worldwide.

Individuals, who're very well skilled in Six Sigma, may be positive to reach excellent decision making and leadership positions inside corporate Ladder.

THE CRITICAL ELEMENTS OF SIX SIGMA

Consumer requirements, layout high quality, metrics and measures, worker involvement and continuous enchantment are most important elements of Six Sigma Procedure Enhancement.

The elementary objective of your Six Sigma methodology may be the implementation of a measurement-based strategy that focuses on process enhancement and variation reduction by way of the application of Six Sigma enchantment projects.

You can find two most important Six Sigma sub-methodologies which are utilized namely the DMAIC and DMADV. The Six Sigma DMAIC procedures means specify, evaluate, evaluate, and strengthen, management. It can be commonly used for improving the program for existing processes falling beneath specification and in search of incremental advancement. The Six Sigma DMADV approach is outline, determine, analyze, layout, verify. It truly is utilized to develop new processes or items at Six Sigma quality levels. It may also be used if a present process requires a lot more than just incremental advancement.

Each of those Six Sigma procedures is executed by Six Sigma Green Belts and Six Sigma Black Belts, and is overseen by Six Sigma Master Black Belts.

The organizations that achieve the greatest advantages from Six Sigma leverage the linkages in between people today, processes, consumer, and tradition.

A Six Sigma defect is defined as anything outdoors of client specifications. A Six Sigma chance is then the total quantity of possibilities for a defect. Process sigma can quickly be calculated making use of a Six Sigma calculator.

Chapter 10: The Foundation Of A Methodology – 5 Stages Of Dmaic

The all-encompassing tool that exists in most Six Sigma project is DMAIC. Mentioned a few times within this book already, DMAIC is the bread and butter for Six Sigma professionals. DMAIC which sounds like, "Duh-may-Ick," is an acronym for the most fundamental Six Sigma method. It stands for Define, Measure, Analyze, Improve and Control, which will walk any professional through the entire process. True to the nature of Six Sigma, the whole process can quickly sum up in a few sentences. This method is put to use during some Six Sigma project to assess every possible aspect leading to defects, then each step, in turn, will produce solutions for defect reduction.

Six Sigma professionals use DMAIC to understand a process that they are known to and to find gaps in knowledge that may be the root cause of underlying problems. This tool plays a role in resolving issues within an organization and within specific operational procedures. You can scale this one tool to assess the entire company or to gain insight into a single process such as filing archived reports.

Dissecting DMAIC is part of building an understanding of Six Sigma methodology and seeing for the first time how it's put into practice. Here you will learn the function and purpose of each phase of DMAIC as well as how to analyze whether you're on the right track for each one or not.

Before diving deep into what each letter of the acronym represents it's worth returning to the original statement. This tool is present in some projects, and not others. DMAIC is all-encompassing, but sometimes it isn't the best tool for the job. One of the many things learned during Six Sigma training is to identify the right tools for each project[24]. To identify if DMAIC is the correct tool to use, you should consider these questions:

● Is there an obvious issue within a particular process?

● Is there an opportunity to reduce time, costs, and productivity within that process?

● Does this situation come with measurable data that is quantifiable?

These questions help you understand if DMAIC steps will apply to your project. Looking a few examples, you'll see that DMAIC is the primary tool used, and can fit into many situations. However, there are always exceptions. Go through this list and see the correlation between using and not using DMAIC.

- Manufacturing floor yield is 'scratching' more product than ever. – DMAIC

- Increase in patient to patient infection rate within a hospital. – DMAIC

- Top-down management restructuring for a culture shift. – No DMAIC

- High employee turnover rate – No DMAIC

- The decrease in day-to-day staff contribution – Possible DMAIC

The primary issue in all of these that listed as "No DMAIC" was that there either isn't driving data, or there isn't enough data. In the top-down management restructuring, you may use many pieces of the DMAIC structure, but you won't use all of it. You won't have real and quantifiable data for how well a leader is taking their new position. Then when you look at the high employee turnover rate example, there are many other factors at play there. A DMAIC approach would fit well if the employees were all from one department.

However, for a company as a whole, it gives a semblance of the need for company-wide changes. That provides a scope with far too big to use DMAIC without having any static data to put to use.

In the decrease of day-to-day staff contribution, it is possible to use DMAIC, but it may not be the best tool for the job. Necessarily, you'll need to pin down precisely what the problem is and then identify if DMAIC fits the role. You'll start the 'define' step to see if DMAIC will work here. It's the same thing as testing a standard screwdriver size to see if it fits the screw you'll work within that moment. "Does this fit?"

Some companies have created another step within the DMAIC process to head off this investigative section called Recognize. However, it's not in line with the official Six Sigma teachings. Within Six Sigma, it's a standard case of putting your skills to work, rather than creating another step, which may be unnecessary.

Define

In the very first step, you're using two mission-critical questions to set out many definitions. First, you'll ask yourself, 'What is the problem?" and then, "How is this problem impacting the company?"

Using these questions to define the problem is, in theory, very simple. However, when put into action shows that things can immediately become spotty and uncoordinated. For example, say a car dealership notices that it has continued to drop in sales throughout the last few months. That's a problem. But it's not the problem. The problem may be that the orders for new vehicles aren't going through or are manually put in with a supplier via phone. The car dealership may have a scorned relationship with their supplier or a particular vehicle manufacturer causing low inventory and low sales. Alternatively, they may have poor customer service review and ratings over the last few years, which are finally impacting their sales figures. Identifying the problem is a challenge that is true to the cliché, easier said than done. So how does someone go about identifying the problem?[25]

During the define phase, you will take a slight sidestep and identify areas for opportunity and identify customer needs. During that point, everyone involved should carefully watch for the real problem. From the example with the dealership above the initial instance of defining might look something like this:

- Black belt professional begins to put the project together.

- Bring in team members and validate the opportunity for improvement.

- Document the business opportunity and outline the scope of the project.

- Identify the stakeholders and craft a team charter for impact.

- Identify all related processes.

- Map related processes.

Many of these tasks are taking place at the same time, and one or multiple of these tasks may lead to the ultimate answer to "What is the problem?" Six Sigma professionals do take care to approach projects with an investigative eye. Think of the way that police should investigate a crime. They should not rule out all other possible suspects or leads just because they have one in custody. An investigation requires exploring possibilities, and that means not stopping because you think you've found the probable problem.

Next, you must answer, "How is this problem impacting the company?" This question fits a vital aspect of the defining process because you're going to start mapping out the procedures as they exist now. That means walking through the process from start to finish with a subject-matter-expert. Usually, a green belt will take on this task. When walking through the process, the Six Sigma professional will carefully document each step and who was involved at any given point.

After identifying the layout of the process and the pain points, the group will work together to define the scope of the project more distinctly. That will impact the group charter, documentation of the business opportunity, and determining which related procedures will see change as well.

The define step will end when the group can bring together a problem statement. A problem statement should encompass the 'When?' 'What?' 'Magnitude,' and 'Consequence.' For example, "In six months we have lost 6% of our repeat customers because shipping was delayed by more than three days or was inconsistent. This impacts 18% of outstanding orders and will negatively affect cash flow." The statement is clear, concise, and leaves little room for misinterpretation.

Measure

After the team leading the project has successfully defined every aspect, you can now start measuring. In a famous quote from Peter Drucker, "If you can't measure it, you can't improve it."[26] That said, the team will start relying on mostly yellow belts at this time to begin collecting, organizing, and analyzing data from any aspect of the company, which impacts the pain points. Gathering the data is vital, and it introduces some key elements of moving forward with the project.

When beginning the measuring stage, there is a bit more of defining necessary, but it all directly fits in with the data used. Key terms and definitions include unit, defect, and opportunity. For many Six Sigma professionals, it is clear what each of these means, but for training yellow belts, it's not.

A unit refers to the smallest measurable element. That could be a single product or a pallet of products. It could be a truck for shipment or an order form. Clearly defining what a unit represents in each project is critical for success. Everyone involved needs a single point of reference, and that is what "unit" refers to.

A defect is another primary term, and it stands in place of the problem with the unit. It can come from any aspect of a procedure or process, and that results in a challenge. Again, as mentioned previously, the defect becomes a concept here rather than a strict definition. In any project, a defect could refer to different problems in different parts of the process. During the measurement phase, this is particularly important. Monitoring and categorizing defects can guide the entire team towards actions, which ultimately reduce all defects.

The final key term here, opportunity, arises out of the defect definitions. When defining what opportunity means to the group and project, you're looking at the process with a positive mindset and looking for a chance to improve. This could mean eliminating a part of the procedure, redelegating the person responsible for any step, or implementing a deviation. It's with the opportunity definition that you start to see how much impact Six Sigma can have within an organization. This defining of opportunity makes many people nervous and can cause some push back across all levels. Six Sigma professionals must bring in their soft skills to bring people on board.

After going through the key terms and understanding what they mean for the project, the team will begin collecting data. The specific data sought after initially is always the DPU, DPO, and P.

DPO stands for Defects per Unit. It's the total number of defects divided by the total number of units. This measurement will help you identify the current standard deviation from the goal of zero defects.

DPU is the Defects per Opportunity, which is one reason why it was so important to define opportunity as a measurable aspect clearly. To calculate the DPU, it is the number of defects/ (number of opportunities per unit x number of units). So first, the person responsible for the measuring would need to identify the number of opportunities per each unit. That's the opportunity to do things correctly and multiply that by the total number of units made. Only then would divide the number of defects by that number.

P is the Proportion defective; it is the number of defective units divided by the total units. This measurement helps people track their mean and identify the progress made on the volume of defects.

As you move forward with each of these equations, you'll start seeing the full scope of your project unfold. Then you'll take this information and start picking apart the functional aspects of each opportunity. To do that you'll move into the next step of the process in measuring and begin writing out a data collection plan.

Data collection plans require that you determine:

• Who will collect the data?

- How frequently that person will collect or update the data

- How many observations are necessary for a fair analysis?

- Whether data should include past, present, or future information

Usually, this process falls to a green belt, and it may be part of the yellow belts ongoing training. They will focus on handling historical data accurately and on setting standardized data. Finally, after all of this, you need to validate your measuring process. To confirm your procedure, you need to test the repeatability, reproducibility, accuracy, and stability. You may realize that each tool or step within the Six Sigma methodology is a "process," which may contain many more processes within it. This setup of nestled processes is standard, and it can help you guarantee that you hit every mark consistently. Essentially the nestled processes eliminate deviation from the success of the tool.

Each step or process has a clear structure, but it's generalized enough to apply to any massive number of situations or projects.

Once you have ensured that your measurement system is valid, then you can focus on building up your output and input relationship. The $Y=f(x)$ relationship is the correlation between the output of the process or Y, and the input or x. This relationship and the formula are more about getting a feel for the opportunities and how you can start changing best practices to improve the process. As you understand this, you'll need to calculate your first Sigma.

The Defects per Million Opportunities is a major milestone in your project and takes place towards the latter end of the measuring process. In this step, you will calculation the Defects per Million Opportunities by simply taking your DPO and multiplying that by one million. But then to create a sigma you'll need to create a standard deviation based on that formula.

The measurement phase is about understanding where you stand currently and taking control of those measurable aspects.

Analyze

Within your measurement phase, you looked at the existing variations within your current process and then compare your goals to your current state. The analysis happens at different levels but does have clear goals throughout the entire process:

Compare the current state to the goal

Recognize variations which lead to inconsistency or defects

Understand the cause behind defects and inconsistencies

Prioritize opportunities to improve

As a natural result of this process, you'll start to find correlations between particular variables and different defects or variations. Many people quickly identify that the variables are not single incidents and often lead to ongoing defects. During every analysis phase, the team will identify KPIVs or Key Process Input Variables. However, this phase allows many other Six Sigma tools to come into action. The team may choose to use a Pareto diagram, a regression analysis, or a root cause analysis. Given that analysis can become subjective and plays a major role in the success of the project, usually the black belt and experienced green belts will determine which tools are best. They will then go through the project helping yellow belts, or fresher green belts put these tools to use.

A particular quote that stands out in acknowledging the transference between the measurement and the analyze phases is that "Quality depends on good data. It also depends on executive leadership in using that data." The Juran Institute[27] published this quote as a way to ease the tension between data collection and change implementation. The middle ground is analysis. Without analysis, you cannot justify the necessary changes, and you cannot have a solid analysis without quality data. You cannot create quality without data or leadership and to obtain both of those you need to establish a clear, concise, and inarguable analysis. It's understandable from the measurement phase that you will continue to collect data, and that the process of data collection won't stop. The analysis step, however, is saying, "We have enough data to do something, so let's see what can be done." When you're analyzing the data and prospects of a project, you will need to include leadership. Few companies are willing to give Six Sigma full control over their processes. It's also poor practice to just deliver a list of demands. Instead, involve higher management and ensure that they approve of all plans. Make sure that they also understand how the team arrived at that analysis and then create a proposed schedule for change implementation.

Unfortunately, much of the analysis phase requires hands-on learning. While you can, and will, learn about the many tools that are present in this step, you can't put any of them into use without a project.

Improve

The team will finally put action into motion with the improve phase. Through the analysis, measurement, and define phases the team brought together the KPIVs, understand the relationships between various aspects of the process and the resulting defects, and you may even understand the root cause of the problem. Now you need to get the backing of the primary stakeholders and propose changes. Change implementation is difficult in every company, in every industry, and on every project. The improve step is what makes soft skills within Six Sigma so critical. An experienced Six Sigma black belt can come into a project, and if they can't obtain the buy-in of leadership, the project won't be successful. What is astonishing to many people is how clear or obvious the 'improve' phase can be for some projects. You may have a good number of peoples saying, "We've been begging for that change for years!" However, that doesn't mean anyone is more on-board. Change is scary, and you're working with people's livelihoods, part of the improve step is making sure that the improvements reach full fruition. Or in other words that no one stops all of the team's hard work before it can even have an impact.

During the improvement phase, the project team will:

- Conduct design of experiments or DOE

- Show results through ANOVA tables

- Develop solutions

- Conduct pilot studies

A lot of the improvement will require you to project your thoughts or theories onto future elements. You may not have data for changing situations, and you may need to work with different Subject Matter Experts to create a cohesive and realistic improvement design. As with the analysis step, you are working out how you can reduce the defects within the given process. That means that you're putting all that prep work to use now.

You will want to start by conducting design of experiments. A DOE is almost always a step in the right direction. Every DOE should highlight the clear relationships or correlations between the outputs and inputs of any process. A process may have many different outputs and inputs within the process map, but all the same, you need to focus on the larger picture. Then you will design factorial experiments where you can change or influence your inputs to impact your output. There is a long list of advanced terminology, which fits into this step, but for a basic overview, we will jump right into the design of a factorial experiment.

During a factorial experiment, you will clearly define the variables you're testing and then use a two-level structure to identify if the process is both effective and simple. You will use those variables with the information you have for each to design for two outputs. At the end of the two-factor testing, you will often choose the output, which will result in the fewest defects, even when it means that the costs are higher on a surface level or that something is more time-consuming. Many Six Sigma projects have proven spending more on a product or during manufacturing can ultimately save the company a substantial amount of money. Why? Because the product is flawless 97% of the time. After your run your DOE, you will show the results on an ANOVA table, which stands for the Analysis of Variance. It allows the group to look at three or more collections of numbers and variances. You can analyze different outcomes or outputs based on materials used, increased efficiency methods, or different process champions.

The ANOVA tables are meant for simple compare and contrast analysis, though. You're using these tables to make improvement decision, and that means that you should be able to identify the complete extent of these changes. Compare how much you expected the changes to the actual outputs. To do this, you will use your f ratio, that Y=f(x), which helps you, see the variances between each group in comparison to the variance of other groups. Ideally, the f will be very close to 1 and prove your hypothesis true. Because of ANOVA tables, you can identify where different variances lead to a very close to 1 f ratio rather than testing one process at a time[28].

The primary tools present throughout the improve phase include the seven deadly wastes, the five S, and even benchmarking. Perhaps the most important and present is the seven deadly wastes. Although waste is not the sole concentration of Six Sigma as it is with

Lean philosophy, these wastes clearly tie together inputs and defects.

As a quick overview, the seven deadly wastes include overproduction, time delays or waiting, defects (clear and avoidable errors such as pricing errors), process inefficiency, transportation, and motion. More on this tool later.

Ultimately the improve phase is about presenting your ideas with the facts, data, and analysis that will sponsor the buy-in of managers and executives. If the data collection was done correctly, then your analysis should be sound, and a sound analysis should lead to well throughout hypothesis[29]. However, even with all of that in play, there is no guarantee that your hypothesis will be accurate. Which is why testing and brainstorming during the improve phase is so crucial.

Control

Although it seems like everything within the DMAIC process is 'the most important' you can argue that everything is for naught if you can't control your solutions. The control step lets you put new procedures or processes into place so that the solutions run smoothly. Control also gives ownership to key people so that they can continue to adapt and optimize the process over time. These key people will need to track data and identify defects, which arise in these processes. No single process is perfect, and no process, which has been reduced to Six Sigma deviation, can remain on that level without maintenance.

As part of your control, you will need to standardize a process, and that requires documentation. The most common documentation includes standard operating procedures, walkthrough, work instructions, and manuals. These documents work on varying levels, and you must identify which is the best fitting for each task or job. Remember that weighing down any particular process with too much documentation can lead to defects as well. For example, if you have a process of baking a cake in which you have a very detailed work instruction, a mildly detailed walkthrough, a thorough standard operating procedure and a manual you can never guarantee that each person baking a cake will use the same document.

You want one document, per step or per process. They should not overlap, but instead, refer the user to the clearest or most succinct document.

During the control as you put together your documentation, the team will craft its implementation plan. That means it will assess a process owner and create a workflow for the entire process. The implementation plan will answer important questions, such as:

• What resources does the process owner need to implement these changes?

• Does the process champion require support from middle, upper, or chief level management?

- Is there a need for multiple Six Sigma advocates?

- Can these changes roll out all at once, or iteratively?

- Is there necessary equipment or software changes, and will those require employee training?

- When will the team begin implementation?

- What is the completion date?

The entire DMAIC process has been building up to the drafting of this implementation plan. In it, you will showcase your data's sway on the analysis and the results of your process testing. There are occasions where you will need to create a response plan for the questions that come your way. A response plan is standard for risk management and can help you overcome foreseeable obstacles without hesitation.

While the DMAIC process seems extensive, it's often completed over the course of only a few days. With a full team on board, various members will take charge of data collection, analysis, testing, and more. Then the team will come together to draft the implementation plan. The DMAIC process is only the beginning of a Six Sigma project.

Six Sigma Success Story

Everyone is familiar with the waiting times that comes with any administrative process. So, it's no surprise to see the full impact of a well-conducted DMAIC in the Los Angeles County Clerk Office. An administrator within the Budget section of the LA County Clerk's office realized that she often completed the same form twice, for the same thing. This form required two signatures from her and required her to complete it on paper and electronically.

After identifying the problem and collecting data, the administrator found that it took forty-three days to complete the form because of the long process of signature collection and request approval. Then the improvement phase showed her that it was possible and plausible to expect the full completion of this form with all signatures and requests completed within just four hours. The implementation plan showed the IT department making this once 15-step document a two-step document that was electronic only. Ultimately, they cut downtime and paper resources as well. The lead time reduction produced a 98% improvement[30]. All because of a well-done DMAIC that took only a few days to complete.

Chapter 11: How Good Is Lean Six Sigma For Small And Medium Size Companies?

The following benefits can be derived by small and medium businesses from Six Sigma:

Providing a standard toolkit to improve business processes

Making processes transparent, manageable

Allowing fact-based decision making

Providing a platform for profitable growth

Aligning organizational and process goals

Helping to establish a focus on the client

Establishing a common language and facilitating communication between people and internal suppliers and customers

Application of Lean Six Sigma

Lean Six Sigma can be linked to the most diverse formations, not just to the engineering ones. Can only engineers take Lean Six Sigma training? Whenever someone asks me this question, I rebut with another question: "Do only engineering students learn statistics during college?" The answer is simple. Of course not, after all, even in a psychology course the student may have contact with statistics. So you mean that anyone can become a Green Belt or Black Belt? Before answering this question let's take a brief reflection.

Engineers are, by definition, people of logical reasoning who use mathematical calculations to turn numbers into efficient processes and functional products. Another ability of your profile is to transfer the ideas from the clipboard to the real world, but for that to happen you also need to have a good understanding of social and economic issues. What I mean is that in the market, there is a very thin line between different areas of knowledge. In practice, every profession has a little of each area, without exceptions.

Let me give you some examples that prove this. A biologist must have knowledge of the social sciences to deal with his patients. A journalist needs to be knowledgeable about the accuracy of interpreting numbers that will give credibility to a story. An engineer needs to know the numbers to understand the social impact of new technology.

And what does this have to do with the Lean Six Sigma methodology? It goes without saying that if you think that only an engineer or an expert in the field of numbers can learn a managerial methodology that involves statistical calculations, you are making a serious mistake. This mistake may cost a better job position in the future, as companies are increasingly looking for multi-disciplinary professionals who are able to solve problems and generate results.

The studies of the last decade have consolidated the definition of the term Lean Six Sigma as a managerial philosophy that allows companies to leverage their profits by improving operations, improving quality, and eliminating defects, failures and process errors. Because it is so broad, this is a methodology that is not restricted to only one area, not least because it is applied not only in the operational sector of companies but also in the administrative areas. Today we have several examples of good results that Lean Six Sigma has brought to the HR, legal, commercial, and even marketing areas of a company. So if in each of these administrative areas, I'm talking about employees with different backgrounds, that is, this methodology is suitable for managers, advertisers, psychologists, economists, engineers, and many other types of professionals. So, anyone can do Lean Six Sigma training? The answer to this question is YES. Anyone can learn and apply the methodology.

The only prerequisite to take on a Lean Six Sigma training is to be willing to face the challenge. It is necessary to know that in the course there is an extensive statistical section that is part of the Six Sigma professional training, but if you are interested in learning to apply the methodology and to face this challenge, you have everything you need to become a professional more valued by the marketplace. Look for stimuli! The ideology of planning is trained in psychology and worked at the core of Human Resources. So it's easy to see: not only engineers or people who work with numbers can learn and apply Lean Six Sigma.

How Can Lean Six Sigma Help Me?

To ensure the success of Lean Six Sigma and therefore ensure its great contribution to achieving results, it is necessary to train people with the appropriate profile and we have already proven here that this does not mean the need for specific training. Duly trained employees will become sponsors of the program and specialists in methodology and quantitative and managerial tools, which will have a great impact in their areas of action and in their chances of reaching new goals and paths. By committing to learning, the consequences will be visible in your activities. Lean Six Sigma can be a possible system for many, just by wanting and having willpower.

Lean Six Sigma in Government Operations

As problems do not distinguish businesses, they occur in the most diverse economic segments and sizes of establishments and in almost every company there is a need for improvements. In the food industry, for example, there may be bottlenecks in the production chain, which can increase the cost of the commodity and generate a number of negative consequences for the organization. In the financial services sector, the difficulty of doing the credit analysis of clients can be an obstacle even to the survival of the business, because this segment is very competitive.

Six Sigma in the Industrial Area

In the industrial area, a manufacturer of auto parts must have a high degree of accuracy to meet the needs of automotive factories. Otherwise, defective items will represent a major loss to the business. In a credit card company, a challenge may be to increase sales to ensure the financial health of the company. Therefore, practically any type of company lives in search of perfecting some process to leverage its own results. What many of them do not know is how to do it.

The differential of Lean Six Sigma methodology in the search for improvements is that it has a very structured method, capable of scientifically proving whether the changes implanted in an organization have in fact resulted in improvement of productivity and quality. Therefore, by having a method, Lean Six Sigma can be applied to different realities with satisfactory results.

When they do not have this methodology, companies tend to want to solve their own production system failures. However, many of them take very inefficient and costly paths to the business, such as putting pressure on employees to get better results. Another unsuccessful way of raising performance is to find scapegoats internally but without any scientific criterion of performance analysis. In such cases, the company walks in circles without finding solutions to its own problems.

By using an improvement road map and using statistical tools to prove or reject hypotheses, the Lean Six Sigma methodology seeks to combine efficiency and effectiveness in the search for better business processes. From the point of view of the projects, it is much more advantageous to invest in this type of work, to solve and to prevent problems, than to bear the consequences of perceived failures by the clients.

Six Sigma in Services

A service provider whose quality is evaluated during the execution of the activity can suffer damages due to defects in the processes. In the case of a bank, if the customer is dissatisfied with something, he can try to solve it at first by self-service, either over the internet or by telephone. If he cannot, he may consider going to an agency to talk to the manager. If this still does not resolve the situation, the customer can complain on consumer protection websites or file a complaint. If all this happens, the banking institution will create a great liability for the institutional image, not counting the possible sanctions of the supervisory entities. Therefore, it is much more advantageous to proactively decrease the rate of complaints than to learn to live with negative results.

Six Sigma in Health Organizations

Other companies that perform closely with their customers are those of telephone companies and those of the health sector. In these cases, the consumer already forms an almost automatic value judgment regarding the enterprise. Therefore, such organizations should be careful not to sacrifice their own business because of a lack of "listening" to complaints and the observation of opportunities for improvement.

In the case of the health sector, the needs of companies are increasing due to a series of factors, such as increase and aging of the population, growth in costs to maintain adequate structure and technology for care, risk of damages to patients, etc. Because this sector deals with the highest good for a person, which is life itself, the degree of excellence in business performance must be enormous.

Over the last few years, various applications of the Lean Six Sigma methodology in the health sector have shown that it is possible to improve three aspects of this area: the care of the population as a whole, the patient's experience in care, and the reduction of costs with the decrease of waste. As you may realize, the Lean Six Sigma approach not only considers economic factors but also customer satisfaction. In the case of the health area, it is not enough for the patient to get treatment for a certain illness, but he must also feel welcomed and cared for.

Six Sigma in the Public Sector

It is necessary to mention that even in the public sector it is possible to have applications of Lean Six Sigma. Entities and government agencies have a great history of dissatisfaction on the part of users of the services. Cases of friction between these parties are common.

In order to overcome this dissatisfaction in the public sector, managers must lead improvement policies in their respective areas of activity, to bureaucratize processes and speed up service delivery. It is clear that proactive initiatives presuppose a certain degree of political will on the part of those responsible for the operation of the public machine, yet they demonstrate that it is possible for Lean Six Sigma to operate in this sector. In Scotland, for example, the model of improvement is a state policy in the country, so it transcends the political plans of some rulers.

Chapter 12: Measuring Data Gaps

Once you are able to define your organization's problems and have created your objectives when it comes to solving them, you are ready to determine what influences the behavior of the process that you wish to improve. To achieve this, you need to enter the Measure phase of Six Sigma's DMAIC methodology.

Measuring performance is considered to be the most time-consuming and difficult part of the DMAIC methodology, but if you do it right, you would be saving yourself from a lot of trouble later on and be able to maximize the improvement that you can create. The way to get the right measurement involves only one way: you need to observe and measure your critical-to-X (known as CTX) characteristics.

Once you do measurement, you will discover that the most important source of problem-solving capability is data.

Using Statistics

Statistics is the process of distilling data, measurements, and numbers in to knowledge and more accurate insight. By understanding how statistics work, you will enjoy leverage using data and use the value of the information that you managed to gather.

Why use statistics? The reason is simple: variation exists in everything, and they greatly reduce your ability to produce quality results, meet schedules, and stay within budget with utmost consistency. Variation is also the reason why any organization commits performance errors. Because variations exist, you have problems to define and you create objective statements to state how you can improve a process.

Of course, until you use science when it comes to getting the results that you want, you will remain in the universe of guesswork, and there lies marginal improvement. No matter how hard you work to achieve improvement, without accurate data, you can only achieve little and unsatisfactory gains.

Statistics may seem to be a terrifying tool for many people who have entered their industries to avoid doing math — but once you collect data using this branch of mathematics, you will get all the support that you need. Once you collect data and measure using statistics right the first time, you will realize that it is not as hard as you think!

Introduction to Measurement

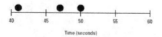

To better understand how you can measure data in a process, here's an exercise: You need to measure how long it takes to fill out a purchase order form. To do that, you need to know how much time has elapsed and then plot it on a horizontal time scale. You can do it like this:

Image source: Six Sigma for Dummies

In this example, the first three measurements are done and the plot shows that it may take 41, 50, and 47 seconds to fill up an order form. However, it does not give you much value – you would need to measure more instances of filling up an order form to see what is likely to happen to the process when done over and over again. Now, when 100 purchase order forms are done, this is how the scale will look like:

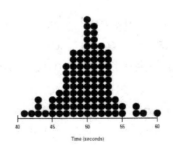

Time (seconds)

Image source: Six Sigma for Dummies

Looking at this scale, similar instances are just stacked up on top of the other. Now, you can see that in this case, it is more likely that people take up 50 seconds to fill up order forms. This image also tells you how the outputs are distributed along the time scale.

Distribution, a statistical term, refers to the way an observable value is likely to occur for a variable factor. You can also call it probability density function, or probability distribution. As you can see in the scale, filling up a form will more probably take up 50 seconds.

Distribution plays a very important role when it comes to creating problem and objective statements for any Six Sigma project because it tells you how a process is performing. Later on, it will also tell you how it can be improved. It leads you to understanding characteristics of the CTXs of your process. In this example, if your output metric is defined as "purchase order completion time", then you have a certain input factor to use.

Measuring Variation Location

Distribution can have infinite points, and in measuring how a process performs, you need to fix a location for the distribution. This will help you find out variations around that location. Statistics will allow you to use three measures of distribution location, which is the following:

Mode

This is the observable value that occurs most frequently and is linked to the highest peak of a distribution. For example, if 10 professionals take an exam and three of them gets a score of 60, three scores 40, and four scores 90, then the mode of 90 occurs more frequently than the other values.

Take note that while using mode is simple and intuitive, this measurement of variation location can cause an error. That is because there are many distributions that do not have a clear peak, and some may have more than one peak. This may prevent you from having a deeper understanding of the variations you want to measure.

2.Mean

Mean is also called the average, and is used as one of the common measures when looking at tendencies of values. The mean is used by many Six Sigma practitioners to make predictions, interpret available data, compare variances, and get a reliable support on what is to be done. The reason is that getting the average of data available makes it possible for one to have a valid prediction of what is likely to happen next.

To calculate for the mean in Six Sigma, use this equation: $\bar{x} = \frac{\sum x_i}{n}$

Wherein:

: (pronounced as ex bar) represents the calculated mean

Σ : Sum of added individual measurements

x_i : Individual measurement values that you wish to add

: Number of individual measurements in your set

Following the given data about filling purchase order forms as illustrated above, you can get the $\bar{x}$ by adding up each value, and then dividing it with its n, which is 100. The result will be 49.9 seconds.

3.Median

The median is that point along the scale wherein half of the data are below and the other half is above. It is also the preferred measure of variation location when the data you managed to collect contains several outliers, or when data points are outside the range variation of other data.

Here is an example: When you want to communicate real estate pricing, you will want to use the median because it is more reflective of the central distribution of prices. If you have a set of properties that have a price of $158,000, $178,000, $535,000, and $125,000, you will get an average price of $239,200.

However, the median will show as $178,000. When you use the median and line up all these prices in a graphical comparison, you will see that the data available has one particular outlier, which is the $535,000 property.

By using the median, you would be able to prevent any potential to contain an outlier data that would bias the calculated mean value.

Using the Mean, Median, and Mode Together

When you use these statistical methods of computing for the variation location, you may still not get the entire story of the variances that you need to measure data. These three measures will all fail to tell you of how narrowly dispersed or how spread out the data is around the central location point.

For example, if you have to sets of data that you intend to measure, and they gave you identical means, the way data is distributed may still differ between them. To ensure that you are measuring the variance location right, you would want to use a second measure. This second measure may also tell you how the data is dispersed around its central location.

The simplest way to measure how data spreads is to use rage. When you refer to the range of the distribution, you refer to the difference between the smallest and the largest observable data value, which you will see by using this formula:

Where:

= calculated range

= largest observable data

= smallest observable data

Going back to the example shown earlier about filling up the purchase order, the range that you are trying to measure is the longest recorded time of filling the form, which is 60 seconds, minus the shortest time, which is 41 seconds. That means that the R for that set of data is 19 seconds.

When you calculate for range, you would get the best results when you compare two measures to even 1,000 measurements. However, it does not tell you about the outliers that much, since data that is well outside the central location is just used as X_{max} or X_{min} in this formula.

Now, if you want to see the distribution's dispersion to get rid of the problem of having data outliers, you would want to look at every recorded measurement and see how far they are from the center of the data set you wish to investigate. This problem is better described mathematically as:

Wherein:

= the single recorded measurement from the data set

= calculated mean of the collected data

The formula $x_i - \bar{x}$ acts as the "score" for each of the data points that you wish to investigate. It works like how scores are calculated in golf – the lower the magnitude of the scores set by a player, the better it is. In statistics, it works better for you because you can see that there are fewer variations in the central location.

Now, there is still a problem here, which you would recognize if you have been dealing with numbers long enough – what if the x_i is smaller than the $\bar{x}$? Keep in mind that you are not interested in finding out whether the data that you are trying to investigate is above or below the line graph when you create a visual representation – you are simply trying to see how far a given value is from the central location.

Having a negative value will only complicate things. To avoid this, you can use the formula $(x_i - \bar{x})^2$ instead to remove the possibility of having a negative value. When you do this, you would be able to penalize points that are farther away from the central value. Take a look at this example:

Image from Six Sigma for Dummies

This figure shows you a plot of how $x_i - \bar{x}$ looks like versus $(x_i - \bar{x})^2$. If an individual point for a data away from the central point, whether it is above or below it, you will see that both $x_i - \bar{x}$ and $(x_i - \bar{x})^2$ gives you a value of 1. However, if the point is twice as far away from the center, you will get a value of 2 with the formula $x_i - \bar{x}$, and a value of 4 with $(x_i - \bar{x})^2$.

Now, you would want to create an overall score for this data set, which you can get by simply adding all the squared scores together. To express that mathematically, statisticians use $\Sigma(x_i - \bar{x})^2$, or summed square error (SSE).

Take note that error does not mean that there is something wrong, at least if you are talking about statistics. The term error refers to the deviation from a comparison value. In the example given above, the error is defined as the difference between the mean and the individual observations.

Once you have totaled the scores, you can find out the typical (or the average) squared score by dividing the SSE by the number of the individual data points that you have collected in this manner: $\sigma^2 = \frac{\Sigma(x_i - \bar{x})^2}{n-1}$, where n refers to the independent points in your collection.

The result of the averaged error score is given the symbol σ^2, which refers to a familiar term "variance." However, while this formula is theoretically useful, you would see that there is a problem here – if you go back to the example of measuring how purchase orders are formed, you are aware that the data that you are collecting, and the result that you want has a measure of seconds.

Now, if you will follow this formula in this scenario, the σ^2 would mean $seconds^2$, which of course, doesn't make any sense.

To get rid of the square sign from σ and go back to the unit of measure that you are trying to use, all you need to do is to get the square root of the result. To do that, you use this formula:

This formula is called the standard deviation formula, which is the most common measure used to see dispersion.

Now that you know how to measure gaps between data that you collect, you would be able to better observe independent values when you collect data. You may also notice that data can change, depending on the length of time that you are trying to observe. At this point, you can put these formulas into action.

Short-term Variations

When you measure short term variations, you would notice that they are occurring in pure random. It may be hard for you to predict what's going to happen next when you are simply observing characteristics of a process in a short amount of time. However, you know that these seemingly random occurrences and characteristics will affect how a process functions in the long run.

The small, observable forces that create changes in the process are called "common". When they cause short-term variations, they are called "common cause variation". Since these seemingly-random variation is still worthy of being quantified by analyzing the differences between characteristic measurements that appear sequential. When you look at the sequential measurement differences, you would see that they are displaying a form of range. When you want to analyze the measurements sequence, or the range (or difference) between the initial two measurements can be thought of as and this leads you to think that the difference between two measurements in a sequence can be written as

and if you want to find the average range between all the points in the sequence, you can simply use the formula: Now, when you want to calculate for short-term standard deviation while looking at a sequence and take the ranges in between points, you simply need to take their average and then multiply the result by a specific factor for correction based on the range found in between two measurements of a sequence. The formula that you can use to do this is:

Using formulas to find a characteristic's standard deviation comes with a warning: you should never try a characteristic's short-term standard deviation unless they are appearing as a set of measurements appearing in a sequence.

Long-term Variation: Where the Shift Happens

Variations that happen in short-term are always bound to change after quite some time. While short-term variations may appear random, you would see that they are bound to shift or drift over time. The bumps and curves, also called disturbances to the process, are detected after some time. When you combine these short-term variations, you would see that these variations are not so random anymore.

When you see the long-term variation, you would be able to see changes in the process, which makes that you detect special causes that influence the process in the long run. Once you are able to detect these special causes, you would be able to make the appropriate changes to your project objectives.

Chapter 13: Identifying Customer Needs

When it comes to trade and industry, the customer is one of the company's most valuable assets. In order to keep customers, the company has to ensure that the customers are happy with the services or goods they are receiving. In order to keep them happy, they must define what customers consider as critical to quality. The company must take into account the service standards that customers demand.

Not only are customers one of the most important aspects of a business, but they are also a very powerful marketing tool for the business. One happy customer will tell at least five other potential customers about their experience, product, and service. This has now made five more potential customers who, in turn, will tell five more; hence, the growth snowballs.

An unhappy customer can do a lot of damage to a business. While a happy customer may brag about how happy they are with a business or recommend it to other people, an unhappy customer has the potential to reach thousands of businesses and people to do the exact opposite. When a customer is on the unhappy spectrum, they tend to want to tell a whole lot more people about their bad experience. If you think about a bad experience you have had with a place, how did you react?

Voice of the customer (VOC) is a tool used by Lean Six Sigma to determine how the customer perceives the service and products they are receiving. This is done by means of surveys, focus groups, meeting with the customer, and so on. The information received from VOC research offers the business a baseline by which to measure the customers' satisfaction or dissatisfaction with a process, service, or product.

This tool also helps the customer identify which products or services need to be investigated in order to find out where they need improvement, where the weak link is that is dragging the product down, or if it is worth continuing with a process, service, or product.

VOC does not just involve the customer; it also involves the workforce of the business. It is not as simple as jotting down some questions and whipping it in the mail to the customer. It requires the following:

1. Management approval and support. In order to run a successful campaign, it needs the support and backing of top management to create a customer-centric project on this scale. However, it is not only the top management that needs to be brought on board. Team leaders and middle management are the leaders who have the most influence over their teams.

2. Planning. A clear and concise vision statement is needed to map out and show what message is being conveyed. What is the scope of the VOC? What is its purpose? What is it going to accomplish?

3. Employee collaboration. Employees of a company are the ones who will ultimately be the driving force in any customer-centric business. They are the ones who know the products, services, and processes better than anyone else in the company. Bringing them in early and getting them involved will ensure the success of the VOC initiative. The workforce can help with the understanding of the product or service. They have valuable input about how the processes work and where they think it could be improved. There are a lot of employees whose skills are being underutilized and who go unnoticed. Keeping the workforce happy, boosting their morale, and showing them that their opinions matter is a sure way to drive the VOC project to success.

4. A common goal within the business. By uniting management, supervisors, and the workforce, the business is set on a common goal. Ensure the customers are

happy and the product or service expectations are met or exceeded.

5. Well-thought-out method for the collection of information and feedback. Based on target customers, products, processes, and services, the business can put together various questionnaires or interviews that will allow them to gather the information they require. It is not only about the gathering of information but also about what is going to be done with the information. What are the baselines on which the information is going to be measured? How will the information be collected? Which customers will need interviews? Which will get surveys? Which products in specific are being targeted? Why?

6. Commitment. The business must be committed from the start of the VOC project and keep up with continuous improvements on their products or services. Being committed to customer satisfaction does not stop at one round of surveys; it is a commitment taken for the

life of the business relationship between the two. It also means that the business is committed to ensuring both the workforce and customers are being heard. The business is the bridge that connects the workforce to the customers. The bridge is only as strong as its support. If one side is not happy, it will cause a ripple effect to the other side. No one wants to navigate or use a rickety bridge.

Determining the Critical Customer Requirements

Customers have a set of critical requirements they look for when choosing a business to supply them with their product or service. A customer wants value for their money, and when they are outsourcing their manufacturing or service provider, they are putting their trust in them to deliver it. There are four main things that a customer looks for. These value quadrants are as follows:

- Cost of the product or service

- Quality of the product or service

- Specified features

- Good turnaround time or availability

Think of yourself as a customer for a minute. You are looking for a coffee shop in which to enjoy your lunchtime coffee each day. There are usually four main things you are going to look for in a coffee shop:

1. Prices (the cost): You are not going to want to pay inflated prices for a cup of coffee. This is something you are going to want to have each lunchtime, so it must be able to fit into your budget.

2. Type of coffee (quality): Like a coffee lover, you are not going to want to spend your time drinking coffee from a tin or that you can buy in any store. You want a good blend, one that is made with care and a barista who knows what they are doing.

3. The menu (features): Does the menu check all the boxes for you? Does it have the selection you were hoping to find in the coffee shop? What is their food like? Are there alternative options should you need there to be?

4. Service (availability): Will they always have the options they advertise available? Do they have good service? How long does it take to get served? What is the service like? Do the management and workforce tend to your needs and make you feel like they are striving to meet your expectations?

The bottom line is customers want a good-quality product or service at a reasonable price and a good turnaround time. They also want to know that the company is aware they exist. They must keep open communication and always strive to exceed customers' expectations.

You know how great you feel when you do get the perfect cup of coffee made by an attentive barista, served with a smile, and then not being forgotten about once the coffee has arrived. You don't want to be interrupted as you are about to take a bite of a muffin or sip of your brew. Any good waiter or manager would wait and watch for the appropriate moment to approach their customers! This ensures repeat business, and of course, the company gets free marketing service when you tell all your friends, colleagues, and loved ones about the coffee shop.

A good manager would also ask you how you were enjoying your food or coffee to gauge your level of contentment with their product and service. This opens up a line of communication, as do their surveys about various aspects of the coffee shop. They usually leave these surveys on a table or on their counters. It may be to rate a new coffee or their service or ask for customers' opinions on how the service could be improved on. They are giving their customers a voice. These surveys or little interviews show the manager whether or not the staff is up to par, the coffee brand is satisfying the customers, and the customers are happy with the cost of the product, especially the regular customers.

A lot of emergency rooms are adopting a new rating service where you can press the red button for bad service or a green one for good service. Not a lot of people may press the green button, and you will find more pressing the red. These ratings give the management a baseline on how to improve waiting time, address understaffing, etc. Maybe even training the staff will be required.

From all the gathered information, the business can work on fixing their processes by cutting out the ones that do not offer value to concentrate on and improving the ones that do. Continuously improving these processes can help keep the current customer base and potentially attract more customers. Always make sure you have asked enough of the right questions!

Chapter 14: What Is Six Sigma?

Many of the concepts that are found with Six Sigma are going to focus on the fields of probability and statistics. You are aiming to answer the question "How confident can I be that what I planned to happen actually will happen?" Six Sigma is going to deal with estimating and after that improving how close we can come to conveying the exact thing that we planned.

However, anything that we do in business, and in other areas, will vary from the plan, even if it's just a little bit. Since no results are able to match our intentions 100%, it is usually going to be seen in terms of a range of acceptability. We allow for a bit of variance, but not for the complete variance, when we come up with a plan for our business. The scopes of worthiness, or our resistance limits, will react to the planned utilization of the result of our works just as the desires and needs of the client.

Quality Can Make Us Stronger

In the past, traditional methods of running a business would say that the higher the quality level, the higher the cost in the long run when compared to the poorer quality. This meant that the company had to raise its prices to provide a higher level of quality, which could make them less competitive. Being able to balance high quality with an affordable and competitive price was the number one key a business had to strive to survive. The surprising discovery of those who started out with Six Sigma is that the best quality doesn't really cost more, and truth be told, it can end up costing less if you use these principles. This is because of a factor known as the cost of value.

Cost of value will be the expense of going amiss from quality and can incorporate paying for things like guarantee claims, scrap, and revamp. Making things directly for your clients the first run through, regardless of whether it requires up more exertion to achieve that abnormal state of execution and quality, a really cost substantially less than making and afterward finding and fixing any deformities that are there.

Six Sigma Steps

There are five steps that we talked about a bit above that are critical to the Six Sigma process. Understanding each of these steps works with Six Sigma can make it easier to implement overall. The steps that your business can take on the way to Six Sigma quality include:

Define

The first thing that you need to do when working on a six sigma project is make sure that

you define the project that you would like to work with. To do this, you must take some time to explore the problem areas that are in your business. It is likely that there are at least a handful of issues that must be taken care of, but you only want to focus on one at a time. Understanding how your business works, and then determining which project is the most important to your success, will ensure that you will get the best results.

The first thing to do is set up some time to observe what is going on in your business. Heck and look at the supply line, how the employees are working, how the products are being replaced, and even customer complaints. Talking to your customers, your managers, and your employees can give you a better idea of what needs to be fixed in your business.

Once you have a list of things that you need to work on, you can rank them in order of which fix is going to provide the biggest improvement to your business. You never want to try and employ Six Sigma on more than one area, or one project, at a time. Doing this is going to get signals crossed, can make it difficult to find enough resources to get it done, and more. Just focus and define one project, the most important project, and put your resources towards that. You can always move on to another problem once you have made the original process more efficient, and reduced the waste there as much as possible.

Measurement

Six Sigma qualities imply that you have to achieve a business standard of committing fewer than 3.4 errors per million chances. This quality would include some of the standards with support, service, administration, marketing, manufacturing, and design. It includes all of the features of the business. Everybody has a similar quality objective and a similar strategy to achieve it. While the application to motor structure and assembling is self-evident, the objective of Six Sigma is execution, and the vast majority of similar devices, likewise apply to the milder and progressively regulatory procedures too.

After the improvement venture has been characterized, the primary procedure of value improvement to measure how well it performs. Effective measurements mean that you need to look at all the problems and processes in a more statistical view. This forces you to rely on data and logic to make sure that you get the quality levels that Six Sigma requires.

To widen the application to a portion of alternate procedures, and to additionally improve the assembling procedure, another definition is useful. Imperfection is something that must be avoided as much as possible and it is going to be an inability to meet a consumer loyalty prerequisite, and the client will at that point be the following individual who appears all the while.

Amid this starting stage, you would need to choose the basic to quality attributes that you might want to improve. This could be founded on an examination of the necessities of your client, with a device like Function Deployment. After you can characterize what principles need to be there for the performance, and you have time to validate the measurement system that you want to use, you would then be able to take a look at your short term and long term goals and how well the process performance is going.

Analysis

The second step in Six Sigma is to characterize the execution goals and afterward distinguish the wellsprings of procedure variety. Most of the time, the execution of all procedures ought to be improved inside five years. This can then be translated into specific objectives.

So, here we need to take some time to identify some of the variations and their causes. After we count the defects, it is imperative that we know when, where, and then how these defects are occurring. Many tools are available that can help to identify the causes of any variations that happen to create these defects.

These can include some of the tools that your business may have seen or used in the past including the histogram, scatter diagrams, fishbone diagrams, run charts, process mapping, and more. Some of these could be brand new to your business, including hypothesis testing, multivariate analysis, box and whisker diagrams, and affinity diagrams.

Improvement

This particular phase is going to involve screening for any of the potential causes of your variations, and then finding out if there is some kind of interrelationship that occurs between them. One of the tools that you will most likely use for this is the DOE or the Design of Experiment. Understanding how these relationships work can help you to set up an individual process tolerance that is going to ensure you get the right results overall.

Control

During the control stage, the way toward approving the estimation framework and afterward assessing its abilities will be rehashed so as to ensure that there was actually some improvement that happened. Steps are then taken in order to control these new processes that are improved. There are a number of tools that are used in this including internal quality audits, mistake proofing, and statistical process control.

A Few Interesting Points about Quality

If you believe that it is just a natural part of running a business to have defects and that quality is going to consist of discovering imperfections, and after that fixing them before these deformities get to your client, at that point you are basically setting your business up for failure. To improve the quality and the speed in your business, you need to be able to measure your process, and you must make sure that you use a measure that is common with them all.

The common business-wide measures that are used in order to drive quality improvement with Six Sigma are going to include absconds per unit of work and process duration per unit of work. These measures will apply similarly no matter what sector you are in and you can use the measurements in support and administration, service, marketing, production, and design.

Everyone in the company, from the top manager to the ones who actually put in the work to make the product, will be responsible for producing quality. This means that everyone measured and accountable for quality. Being able to measure the amount of quality within an organization, and then pursuing an aggressive rate of improvement - is going to be the responsibility of the operational management in this system.

Always remember the customer during this process as well. Customers want a product that is delivered on time that works right when they get it, they want to avoid any failures within the first few weeks or more of owning the product, and they love products that are reliable over the lifetime of that product. If the process you use is allowed to make defects, then it is hard to save the customer from these defects just by some simple inspections and testing.

A design that is robust, or one that is well inside the capacities of existing procedures to deliver it, will be vital to making sure that you reduce costs while increasing the amount of satisfaction that your customers have with you. The best approach to locate a hearty plan is through the simultaneous building of incorporated structured forms. Since having higher quality in your products is going to ultimately reduce the costs, the most elevated quality produce is most ready to be the least dimension cost maker, and this makes them the best rival in the market with their products.

Implementation of the Six Sigma Methodology

The choice to take Six Sigma and implement it is going to depend on whether you are trying to improve an existing process or if you are trying to create a new process or product from scratch. If you are working on improving one of the processes that you already have, you will work with the DMAIC that we talked about before. But if you need to improve a new process or product design, you would work with DMADV.

DMAIC

When we are working with Six Sigma, the DMAIC methodology is going to involve defining improvement goals, measuring what standards are already in place at a baseline future reference, and then analyzing the relationship between any of the defects that are there and the things that cause these effects to show up.

This method is also going to entail working to improve processes in order to deliver consistent goal achievement in accordance with the strategy that the company already has in place. The method is also going to make sure that any changes you make are going to still be consistent with the demands you get from the customers. The analysis process of this method is going to set the stage for the corrections that you need, called the improvement.

DMADV

In addition, you can use the Six Sigma process to help create new processes for product development. This is going to be slightly different in the final two stages of the process because you are dealing with a brand new process or product, rather than one that has been used for some time. Defining and measuring the design and the product goals, as well as the capabilities of the product will be the two stages you start with.

The next stage is going to include analyzing alternatives and then evaluating to make sure that you go with the product design that is the best. Once you make that design, you will need to implement the one that you chose. The final step means that you need to verify the design, pilot or test out the product a few times and then testing implementation before you complete the final presentation.

There are several big organizations, including Motorola, Microsoft, GE, and the United States Navy who were able to implement Six Sigma with new products and they saw huge success. However, implementing this is going to require that the organization is able to play 5 key roles at different levels. At the top is going to be the executive level. This level is going to include the CEO, the champions, and then the black belts and master black belts. Then there are the green belts or the individuals who will dedicate 100 percent of their efforts toward the concerted implementation of the program until it reaches the end.

Things that Six Sigma Is Not

While we have spent some time talking about what Six Sigma is, let us now know a few of the things that this method is not. Some of the things that Six Sigma isn't, or that it doesn't offer in its employment will include:

It is not a prevailing fashion. There is a huge amount of publicity about the procedure, however, this is basically on the grounds that it really works, rather than just being a fad. When it is used in the proper manner, it can be beneficial to many different types of businesses, and because it is so effective, it is probably going to be around for quite a while.

Six Sigma is not the arrangement. With the right training, you will discover that this procedure improvement is the way to finding the arrangement, as opposed to being the genuine arrangement all alone. Try not to consider it to be the appropriate response you have to get from the issue, however a way to take care of the current issue.

These ventures aren't only for huge companies. You can utilize this strategy in practically any limit, as long as the correct preparing standards are connected. Business visionaries and even independent companies can utilize Six Sigma to guarantee their business is progressively successful overall.

It is not another or an improved adaptation of the absolute quality administration. These two processes are similar, but they aren't the same. Tool Quality Management is going to focus on the final product and the procedure improvement. Six Sigma is going to focus on business achievement and furthermore improving the odds that achievement is going to occur on a big and large scale.

It is not going to be for everyone. Even though this method seems all-encompassing, in some cases, it is not going to be the right choice for a solution. You must be able t identify the problem and its cause, and then decide whether Six Sigma or another choice is the right choice for eliminating the problem.

Any business that needs to make the most out of Six Sigma must almost certainly comprehend what this strategy is. To get a smart thought of what Six Sigma is, you have to know more about how it works, as well as more about what it isn't. When you leave on the way to Six Sigma preparing, ensure that you begin with a receptive outlook and that you never pre-judge the process without first taking the time to learn everything there is about this methodology.

Chapter 15: Running A Project With Kanban

When setting out to incorporate Kanban into a project, it's important to note that the project itself does not have an iterative nature under the Kanban methodology. Rather, Kanban is a type of workflow management system that enables you to carry out tasks in a sequential and linear manner. As a result, your task flow management becomes much more efficient, thereby enabling you to reduce time and waste.

How so?

The reason for this is that Kanban isn't an iterative methodology in the way that Scrum is. As such, the way a project is run under the Kanban principle is meant to be incremental. So, one task gives way to another, and so on. As we have stated earlier, there is a clear need for one task to be cleared off the Board before another can begin. If there are too many tasks on the Board at the same time, then the project may end up falling behind schedule.

It's important to note that a Kanban has one beginning and one end. Unlike Scrum, there are no sprints. There are, however, cycles. Each cycle is completed every time a User story is done. When a User Story is completed, the customer can be summoned to get an update on the process of the project. Thus, the beginning of the project is marked by the official kickoff while the end of the project is marked when the customer gives the final "okay."

Getting Started with a Kanban Project

Kanban-based projects start out pretty much like any other project. There is a customer that want something done and a project team that can do it. Just like Scrum, the customer can be external or internal, depending on the dynamic of the project.

Here is where things diverge somewhat from Scrum. In a Kanban project, there is the leader of a "project manager" who is the owner of the project, so to speak. The project manager is tasked with being the person who coordinates the administrative side of the project. Unlike the Product Owner, the project manager may be an internal stakeholder who is responsible for ensuring the project gets done.

The project manager is responsible for producing the project charter and any other relevant documentation that may be needed as part of the project's governance. Please bear in mind that documentation ought to be kept to a minimum. So, only the required paperwork should be put together in order to make sure the rules of the game are clear.

Then, the project manager can go about searching for a Service Request Manager. The SRM can be an additional person that is dedicated solely to the project itself, or the project manager can double up in this role. In fact, it makes a lot more sense for the project manager to double up in this role as it means that there is one less line of reporting. This reduces the time wasted among the various interlocutors communicating. As such, this concept diverges from Scrum as the stakeholders, and Product Owners are different individuals. In Kanban, it doesn't really matter, especially when stakeholders are keen on ensuring the project gets done.

The project manager, or SRM, is then in charge of defining the project's scope and deliverables. By sitting down with the customer, the project manager can determine what needs to be done. This workflow management leads to the creation of User Stories. The User Stories, just like Scrum, are the description of the end users who will interact with the final outputs delivered by the project. In the end, the User Stories create the project Backlog. The Backlog is comprised solely of

User Stories as tasks are determined far along on by the project team.

Once the scope of the project and User Stories have been defined, the project manager can go about assembling the project team. It should be noted that there is no prescribed number of team members, as is the case in Scrum. The number of team members can be as high as it needs to be. In fact, large projects work well under Kanban as there is no restrictions in the dynamic of the workflow. Since Kanban is sequential in nature, the project manager can simply go about determining what needs to be done and how many people need to do it.

As such, the project manager needs to be an experienced individual in the project's field. The project manager needs to understand the needs of the tasks that will be completed in order to determine how long tasks will take and how they should be completed. While the project team has the freedom to determine their workflow, the project manager needs to be the guide for the overall tempo of the project.

Assembling the Team

As mentioned earlier, the project manager is tasked with bringing the team together. Since the project manager is the main interlocutor with the customer, they cannot be fully immersed in the project. This means that they cannot have a functional role within the project team through the project manager may be able to contribute any way they can.

The profile of each team member needs to fit the needs of the project. So, if the team is building a house, there is a need for plumbers, masons, electricians, carpenters, and so on. The actual number of each type of member is determined by the overall scope of the project. As such, a small project would require a smaller number of members, while a large project would require a larger team.

On the whole, the project team is self-regulating. This means that they are able to distribute the workflow as they see fit. This means that team members are encouraged to rotate from task to task so long as they are able to complete them in a timely manner. The last thing that you want to have is a rigid structure in which everyone is typecast into a role they cannot get out of. By fostering collaborative communication, the team can determine who does what and when.

Although, it should be noted that the project manager has the official ruling in which User Stories are prioritized. The prioritization of the tasks related to that User Story depends on the project team. The thing that matters is that each individual task is completed within the allotted time (time boxing) and that the User Story is completed within the timeframe established at the outset of the project.

As for the Service Delivery Manager role, the SDM ought to be a project team member that is doubling up on this role. Since the main purpose of this role is to ensure quality and continuous improvement, it makes sense to have a team member perform this role. Of course, this role has no authority, so it's not meant to be a "boss" that supervises everyone else. If you wanted to go about this role democratically, you could rotate the position among members who are qualified and willing to do it. This divides up the responsibility and does not place the burden solely on one person.

Divvying Up Time

Since Kanban is sequential, time is managed by determining how long individual tasks ought to take. So rather than fitting X number of tasks in X amount of time, X amount of time is assigned to X number of tasks. This means that the time needs to be cognizant of how much time they really need to get things done. That's why it's a good rule of thumb to overestimate task time by around 20%. If there is ever any time leftover, this time ought to be allocated to testing. Please keep in mind that testing is of the utmost importance under the scope of an Agile-based project.

As for the number of days and hours that a project team plans to work, this is determined by the team itself. This means that the team needs to figure out how much time they are going to devote to individual tasks. Once a task is completed, they can move on to the following. Doubling up on tasks, or multitasking is discouraged as this can lead to the "In Progress" column getting jammed.

Lastly, it's worth noting that since Kanban focuses on incremental progress, cycles will never be distributed evenly. As such, some cycles may take longer than others. This is something that the customer needs to be aware of.

Project Cycles

In short, a project cycle refers to the transition of a User Story from Backlog all the way to the "Completed" column. The overall cycle is determined by the User Story going from a sketch to a working piece of kit. This is when the customer can see what the team has produced at every stage of the process.

Here are the main stages of the cycle:

Backlog. The User Stories are created by the project manager and assigned to the Backlog. Depending on the nature of the User Stories, the project manager may decide to prioritize one story at a time, or perhaps tackle multiple stories simultaneously so long as the project team is able to handle it.

Planned. At this point, the project team comes together to plan how the User Story will be completed in terms of the tasks that need to be done. Work is divided up and assigned to individual team members. The SDM can be named at this point and tasked with keeping track of time.

In progress. The User Story is moved to this column along with all the cards that correspond to the tasks in progress. The SDM needs to ensure that the Board is updated constantly as tasks are completed and moved on to the following column. It should be noted that anything that is still being worked on is in progress.

Developed. The finished task is considered to be developed when there is no additional work needed on it. Then, the card is moved to this column while the task waits for it to be tested.

Tested. Generally, there is a testing team that is assigned to this task. The testing team should only test as many tasks as they have the capacity for. Often, they cannot test multiple tasks a time; this means that they might need to test one task at a time. Once the tasks have been tested and pass criteria, the card can then be moved to this column. When all tasks have been tested, and the complete User Story has been tested out, the User Story card can be moved to the "Tested" column.

Completed. Lastly, once all the testing has been completed and the customer gives the green light, the User Story can be moved to the "completed" column. Individual tasks that have been developed, tested, and approved also go to this column.

Chapter 16: Six Sigma Tools

Within this chapter, we are going to go over several of the best tools that you can use when making use of the lean Six Sigma methodology. Consider that this is by no means an exhaustive list—there are many, many different tools that you can use throughout the DMAIC process. However, these are some of the best places to get started. As you go through this list, keep in mind that tools are organized by the stage of DMAIC that they are usually utilized within. The Define tools, for example, are typically utilized during the Define step in the process, and so on. When you make use of these tools, they can really help you facilitate the changes that you are trying to make, the successes that you really want to implement and help you see the results that ultimately matter most to you. These tools should be useful to you, but feel free to take a look at other tools as well that may benefit you in the long run.

Define Tools

Project Charter

Your project charter is going to be a sheet that you can record all of the information that you are going to find is relevant during this entire DMAIC process. You are looking at the problems that you are currently having with your system, the goals, the timelines, and everything else. You are ultimately trying to put down all of the information than any newcomer to the project would be able to look at and understand exactly who is doing what at any given time.

Designing your charter can happen in any way that you really want to do so. However, there are a few recommended categories that you should include:

The problem statement: This should address questions about the problem that you are having. Ask yourself what is not working at the moment and when that is happening. Ask yourself how often these problems are arising and what the ultimate repercussions to this are. You are going to want to know about the personal and the financial impacts of this problem to keep them in mind.

The business case and benefits: This should address questions about why this project matters. Ask about why this problem is worth solving and why it is worth solving right that minute. How is it important, and what will happen if you do not solve it? Does this project fit in with any other initiatives or targets that you are trying to hit?

The goal statement: This is where you identify what you want. Usually, this will be to either increase or decrease something from a baseline of whatever your base measurement is to a very specific target with a very specific end date to the project to allow you to set an ultimate failure point if nothing actually gets changed.

Timeline: This is where you figure out when you plan to complete each of the DMAIC steps, as well as where you can record the actual time of completion for each step.

Scope: This is going to help you figure out what you are putting into a project, as well as what you are going to get out of it.

Team members: This is a list of everyone that is going to be participating in this project as well as the roles that they are playing, so everyone knows in advance who is going to be doing what. When you have this all lined out in this manner, you are then able to avoid running into future complications about who did what and whose job it really was.

Swim Lane Map

This is a process map—it will allow you to separate your processes into lanes that are meant to represent different steps, functions, or people. It is usually referred to as a swim lane because it appears like a swim lane—each lane will be representative of a different person, and it will allow you to sort of visualize the process for yourself.

Let's say that you have Alfred and Bob working on a project. Alfred is in Lane One, and Bob is in Lane Two. Alfred has to do steps 1, 3, and 5 of the project while Bob does 2, 4, and 6. You are then able to set up a chart that is horizontal—you can put Alfred on top and Bob on the bottom. You will then create squares on the chart for steps 1-6 and then place them in the relevant lane, but done in chronological order.

This is something that can really help people visualize who is going to be doing what, and there are many different tools online that can help you create one of these.

Stakeholder Analysis

Another tool that can really help you figure things out is a stakeholder analysis.

This can help you by allowing you to create a functional outline of who has an interest in your process and why it matters to them. This will help you figure out how much these people will be impacted, how much support they have and why they support or disapprove of the changes that you are trying to make and the actions that will help you meet the desires of these people or the actions that you will need to take in order to figure out how best to address them. Finally, you will want to include some contact information, so you have it all available at a glance.

With this, you are best served just creating a large chart with a category for the stakeholder, the level of impact you will have on them, the level of support, the justification for that support, or lack thereof, the actions that you will take, and finally their contact information. Then, just fill it in as you go.

Measure Tools

Data Collection Plan

The data collection plan is going to provide you with a simple way that you will be able to organize all of the data that you are actively recording at any time. This can help you measure out what is going on so you can then begin to understand how it is impacting everything at large.

This is essentially just a chart that you will use with notes on it that you can use to figure out precisely what you are doing with each study that you are collecting.

You will essentially want to create several different categories here—these categories will allow you to figure out whether your process is going to work out for you at the end of the day. Consider recording the following information on your chart:

The title of measurements: This could be how often an order is messed up, or how long it takes someone to do something. The catch here is that you will want to label precisely whether the measurement is something continuous or if it is something defined, such as the numbers or orders missed versus the varying and continuous-time that it will take for you to be able to define the time.

The operational definition: This is going to provide you with precisely what it is that you are looking to order. In a sentence, that is easy to understand for anyone that looks at it. This could be, for example, "The number of times the computer crashed while using that new program."

How often is this being reported and by whom: This is going to help you understand when data is going to be collected—it will tell you the who, what, where, and when this will happen, so you know what to expect.

How often you will go over the information: This is all about how often you will collect your data and actually consider it. This could be that you spend several weeks trying to record something, or you ask every x customers how their experience was.

Operational definitions

Operational definitions are a great way for you to line everything up, so everyone is on the same page, no matter what happens or how people wind up interpreting it. Think of this as naming all of the possible variables that you can encounter, no matter how simple or straightforward it might sound. That straightforwardness is not the problem here—you are trying to ensure that there is no room for confusion or error in understanding.

You will essentially write down the measurement that you will be taking and then defining it. If you were to write down "Occurrences of crashing," for example, you would then define it as, "The number of times that the computer crashed when using that one specific program that is being analyzed."

Analyze Tools

Charts

Charts of any kind are great for you to use when you are at the analyze stage. This will help everyone understand what is going on and how you can then begin to implement it elsewhere. When you do this, you know that you are setting everyone up with a sort of visual of what is going on so everyone can be on the same page. This is critically important—when you use a chart, you know that everyone sees the same data in the same place.

To up this efficiency, you should also consider making use of at least two ways of presenting the information every time that you do to ensure that it is thoroughly understandable for everyone involved. This means making sure that you are not only showing a chart but also writing out the results that are shown on the chart.

Sometimes, that change in perspective can really make a difference and help you ensure that everyone is, in fact, on the same page. When you have those different perspectives as well, you also have the benefit of wording things in ways that may very well help people consider the data differently, which could allow them to see different patterns that may be of use to you.

Root Cause Hypothesis

The major part of the analysis stage is all about ensuring that you can properly juggle several hypotheses, it can really help to come up with a handy chart that will allow everything to be processed and laid out in front of you for future reference. In this case, you are going to be considering several different hypotheses at once and tracking them all on a nice, handy chart. Keep in mind that this chart is going to hold the bare-bones information for you, and you may want to ensure that you keep a more detailed analysis of this information elsewhere as well.

For this, you will make a table with plenty of room for writing. You will want to write down the following categories:

The possible cause of the problem: Try to keep this in as short of a blurb as possible. If you can cut it down to just one or two words, great. Remember, you can have more information written down elsewhere—this will act as a sort of table of contents for the information that you are recording and processing.

The hypothesis: This is the theory of how the possible cause is influencing the project. In this instance, you could say that the computers are all crashing because they are too old to run the program that is being put on them.

The validity of the claim: Here, you will either record that it was true or false.

The verification: Here, you will write down how you proved or disproved it. This should be short—you will write down the data that you collected to verify one way or the other and then try to summarize it for yourself.

The Five Whys

This is a chart where you can sort of summarize up a bunch of information. In this tool, you are going to simply be asking why something happened or why it had certain results over and over again. Think of this as trying to get to the bottom of a situation to ensure that you know precisely what is going on with it.

Let's consider the example of not meeting production values. You will ask why to the previous answer—and you will do this five times, such as:

Why is production low?

Because there is a lot of downtime where nothing is happening

Why is there downtime?

Because the computers keep crashing and no one can do anything when they are not running

Why are they crashing?

Because we are trying to run a certain program that you asked us to use

Why is this program crashing the system?

Because the computers are not powerful enough

Why do we have computers that are not powerful enough?

Because no one has bothered to replace them in years, and they are now obsolete.

With this example, you have just gone through several questions to figure out a potential cause of the problem. While the data may have looked like the problem at hand was that no one was working hard enough to ensure that they are getting their work done on time, it actually appears that there may have been an underlying cause to that, which quite possibly would have gone entirely ignored had someone not pointed it out in this sort of line of questioning.

Improve Tools

Brainstorming

One of the greatest tools that you can use in the Improve stage is brainstorming. This is simply getting several people to work together to attempt to figure out how to solve a challenging situation. This is not always necessary—for example, in the previous example given with the obsolete computers, there is a very easy solution: You replace the computers. However, when met with more of a challenge, where no solution seems obvious, brainstorming can help everyone work together to come up with the best possible solution.

It is important to remember that during this stage, there should be nothing but thinking and innovation. If a plan seems impossible to implement, worry about that later—for now, entertain it and record it. You can come up with those criticisms later on when you try to figure out how to implement it.

Pilot checklist

The pilot checklist is going to be your checklist that you build up that will help you figure out precisely how to implement that new change that you are aiming for. When you do this, you are able to allow for the process to be better regulated because you have everything all lined up for yourself, nice and neatly. When you do this, then, you are going to want to consider the following categories for your plan:

The strategy: What are you planning on changing? What are the important details about that strategy that you are changing in the first place?

The training prep: What has to happen to get everyone on the same page to ensure that everyone is able to succeed with ease? How can you make that happen? What are the steps?

The measurement: How are you going to be recording whether or not these methods are working for you?

The adjustment plan: How are you going to be making changes, and how do you foresee them impacting the situation at hand?

Implementation Plan

The implementation plan is very similar to the pilot checklist, but it will require the use of several actions rather than the use of a planning list. This is going to be nothing but the necessary steps and how it is responsible for implementing them. You are going to want to record each and every step that has to happen, one by one. Then, you want to record who is responsible for making that action happen. Finally, you want to record the deadline that they have to make it happen, when does it absolutely have to happen to ensure that everyone is successfully able to implement this plan?

Conclusion

let's hope it was informative and able to provide you with all of the tools you need to achieve your goals. Just because you've finished this book doesn't mean there is nothing left to learn on the topic; expanding your horizons is the only way to find the mastery you seek. Additionally, it is important to keep in mind that, while there is some overlap between any two startups, much of what is going to take place is going to be largely unique to the startup in question.

After all, isn't the point of a startup to do something new? As such, it is important to understand that while following the Lean Startup strategy can certainly lead to success, sometimes you may have to make your own way because what you are trying to do is so out there that the existing methods of testing don't apply. This doesn't mean that you should abandon all that the Lean way of doing things has done for you thus far, it simply means that you will need to take what you have learned and use that to create logical ways to test whatever it is you are prototyping. Likewise, it is important to not get impatient and try to rush the process. After all, creating a viable product or service that a targeted portion of the audience is interested in is a marathon and not a sprint which means the slow and steady wins the race.

CPSIA information can be obtained
at www.ICGtesting.com
Printed in the USA
BVHW051029291021
620251BV00012B/255